SMP interact

18

D1079090

Foundation

1

practice

for **AQA, Edexcel** and **OCR two-tier GCSE mathematics**

CAMBRIDGE
UNIVERSITY PRESS

The School Mathematics Project

Writing and editing for this edition John Ling, Paul Scruton, Susan Shilton, Heather West
SMP design and administration Melanie Bull, Pam Keetch, Nicky Lake, Cathy Syred, Ann White

The following people contributed to the original edition of SMP Interact for GCSE.

Benjamin Alldred	David Cassell	Spencer Instone	Susan Shilton
Juliette Baldwin	Ian Edney	Pamela Leon	Caroline Starkey
Simon Baxter	Stephen Feller	John Ling	Liz Stewart
Gill Beeney	Rosemary Flower	Carole Martin	Biff Vernon
Roger Beeney	John Gardiner	Lorna Mulhern	Jo Waddingham
Roger Bentote	Colin Goldsmith	Mary Pardoe	Nigel Webb
Sue Briggs	Bob Hartman	Paul Scruton	Heather West

CAMBRIDGE UNIVERSITY PRESS

Cambridge, New York, Melbourne, Madrid, Cape Town,
Singapore, São Paulo, Delhi, Mexico City

Cambridge University Press
The Edinburgh Building, Cambridge CB2 8RU, UK

www.cambridge.org
Information on this title: www.cambridge.org/9780521689991

© The School Mathematics Project 2007

First published 2007
Reprinted 2013

Printed in India by Replika Press Pvt. Ltd.

A catalogue record for this publication is available from the British Library

ISBN 978-0-521-68999-1 Paperback

Typesetting and technical illustrations by The School Mathematics Project
Other illustrations by Chris Evans
Cover design by Angela Ashton
Cover image by Jim Wehtje/Photodisc Green/Getty Images

Using this booklet

This booklet provides well graded exercises on topics in the Foundation tier up to the level of GCSE grades D and E. The exercises can be used for homework, consolidation work in class or revision. They follow the chapters and sections of the *Foundation 1* students' book, so where that text is used for teaching, the planning of homework or extra practice is easy.

Even when some other teaching text is used, this booklet's varied and thorough material is ideal for extra practice. The section headings – set out in the detailed contents list on the next few pages – clearly describe the GCSE topics covered and can be related to all boards' linear and major modular specifications by using the cross-references that can be downloaded as Excel files from **www.smpmaths.org.uk**

It is sometimes appropriate to have a single practice exercise that covers two sections within a *Foundation 1* chapter. Such sections are bracketed together in this booklet's contents list.

Sections in *Foundation 1* that do not have corresponding practice in this booklet are shown ghosted in the contents list.

To help users identify material that can be omitted by some students – or just dipped into for revision or to check competence – sections estimated to be at national curriculum level 4 are marked as such in the contents list and as they occur in the booklet.

Marked with a red page edge at intervals through the booklet, there are sections of mixed practice on previous work; these are in corresponding positions to the reviews in the students' book.

 Questions to be done without a calculator are marked with this symbol.

Questions marked with a star are more challenging.

Answers to this booklet are downloadable from **www.smpmaths.org.uk** in PDF format.

Contents

continues >

1 Reflection and rotation symmetry

You need triangular dotty paper for section C and squared paper for section F.

c Both types of symmetry

1 (a) Copy this shape and draw all its lines of symmetry.

(b) What is its order of rotation symmetry?

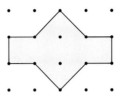
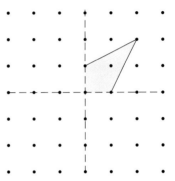

2 (a) Copy and complete this diagram to make a shape where the dotted lines are lines of symmetry.

(b) Draw **all** the lines of symmetry on the completed shape.

(c) Write down the order of rotation symmetry of the completed shape.

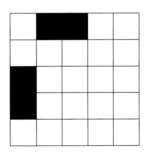

3 (a) Copy this diagram.
Shade four more squares so that the diagram has rotation symmetry of order 4.

(b) How many lines of symmetry has the completed diagram?

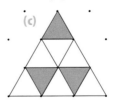

4 Copy each of these shapes on to triangular dotty paper.

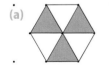 (a)   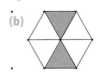 (b)   (c)   (d)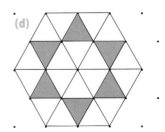

For each shape,

(i) draw in any lines of symmetry

(ii) write the order of rotation symmetry underneath

D Special triangles and quadrilaterals
E Symmetrical and regular polygons

1 (a) What is the missing word in the statement below?

The octagon has been split into three quadrilaterals:
a rectangle and two identical ....

(b) In this design, the same octagon has been
split into two identical shapes.

(i) What is the name of each of these shapes?

(ii) What is the order of rotation symmetry
of the whole design?

(iii) How many lines of symmetry does it have?

2 How many sides has a decagon?

3 Draw a rhombus and show all its lines of symmetry.

4 What is the name of a polygon with six sides?

5 What sort of triangle is being described each time?

(a) It has two equal sides.
It has one line of symmetry.

(b) It has no sides that are equal.
It has no reflection symmetry.

(c) It has three equal sides.
It has three lines of reflection symmetry.

6 (a) Draw a parallelogram.

(b) How many lines of symmetry does your shape have?

7 One of these shapes is a regular polygon.
Which one is it?

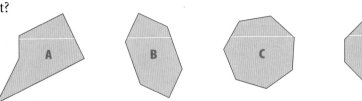

8 (a) Draw a pentagon with only one line of symmetry.

(b) Draw a quadrilateral with rotation symmetry of order 2.

*9 Draw a hexagon with two lines of symmetry.

F Using coordinates

1 Each shape in this diagram is one half of a polygon. Each one has line M as a line of symmetry.

Copy the diagram.

(a) Draw in the rest of each shape after reflection in line M.

(b) Write down the coordinates of each corner of the kite.

(c) Write down the name of the other shape.

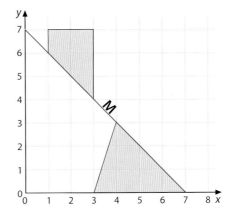

2 This diagram shows half of a shape that has rotation symmetry of order 4.

(a) Copy the diagram and complete the shape.

(b) Name the completed shape.

(c) Write down the coordinates of each corner.

(d) Show all the lines of symmetry on your diagram.

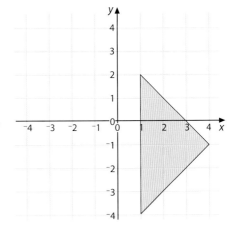

3 Draw a grid going from ⁻4 to 4 on both axes.

(a) Plot the points $(1, 2)$ and $(1, {}^-1)$.

(b) **(i)** Add another point to make a right-angled isosceles triangle.

   (ii) What are the coordinates of this point?

(c) Show any lines of symmetry on your triangle.

4 This diagram shows half of a hexagon that has rotation symmetry of order 2.

(a) Copy the diagram and complete the shape.

(b) How many lines of symmetry has the hexagon?

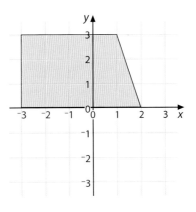

2 Fractions

1 The diagrams show two equivalent fractions.
   What fractions are they?

2 Copy these and find the missing numbers.

(a) $\frac{1}{2} = \frac{\blacksquare}{8}$ (b) $\frac{2}{5} = \frac{\blacksquare}{15}$ (c) $\frac{3}{4} = \frac{\blacksquare}{16}$ (d) $\frac{3}{8} = \frac{15}{\blacksquare}$ (e) $\frac{4}{7} = \frac{16}{\blacksquare}$

3 Write each of these fractions in its simplest form.

(a) $\frac{6}{10}$ (b) $\frac{5}{15}$ (c) $\frac{12}{18}$ (d) $\frac{12}{20}$ (e) $\frac{9}{21}$

4 Write, in its simplest form, the fraction of each square that is shaded.

(a)   (b)   (c)   (d)

5 (a) Which fractions in the loop are equivalent to $\frac{1}{3}$?

   (b) Which fractions in the loop are equivalent to $\frac{2}{5}$?

   (c) One fraction is left over.
        What is the simplest form of this fraction?

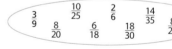
$\frac{3}{9}$ $\frac{10}{25}$ $\frac{2}{6}$ $\frac{14}{35}$ $\frac{8}{20}$ $\frac{6}{18}$ $\frac{18}{30}$ $\frac{8}{24}$

*6 Which fraction is larger, $\frac{6}{24}$ or $\frac{3}{15}$?
    Use equivalent fractions to explain how you decide.

D Mixed numbers

1 Change these improper fractions into mixed numbers.

(a) $\frac{13}{5}$ (b) $\frac{5}{3}$ (c) $\frac{12}{7}$ (d) $\frac{13}{6}$ (e) $\frac{19}{8}$

2 Arrange these fractions in order of size, smallest first.

   $\frac{14}{3}$ $\frac{13}{6}$ $\frac{12}{7}$ $\frac{13}{4}$ $\frac{10}{5}$

3 Write each improper fraction as a mixed number in its simplest form.

(a) $\frac{6}{4}$ (b) $\frac{10}{6}$ (c) $\frac{25}{10}$ (d) $\frac{26}{8}$ (e) $\frac{33}{15}$

E Writing one number as a fraction of another

In these questions, write each fraction in its simplest form.

1 Patrice took 24 photos on holiday.
16 of the photos were of people. The rest were of places.
What fraction of Patrice's photos were of people?

2 Six children in a class of 30 are left-handed.
What fraction of the class are left-handed?

3 Class 10R consists of 12 fourteen-year-olds and 20 fifteen-year-olds.
What fraction of the class are fourteen-year-olds?

4 A hotel has 20 double rooms and 5 single rooms.
What fraction of the rooms are single?

5 Josie keeps rabbits.
She has 12 white rabbits, 10 brown rabbits and 8 black rabbits.
What fraction of her rabbits are

   (a) white   (b) brown   (c) black

F Adding and subtracting fractions
G Multiplying a fraction by a whole number

1 Work these out, simplifying where possible.

   (a) $\frac{2}{5} + \frac{1}{5}$ (b) $\frac{2}{9} + \frac{5}{9}$ (c) $\frac{3}{7} - \frac{1}{7}$ (d) $\frac{3}{7} + \frac{3}{7}$ (e) $\frac{7}{11} - \frac{5}{11}$

   (f) $\frac{5}{6} - \frac{1}{6}$ (g) $\frac{5}{8} + \frac{1}{8}$ (h) $\frac{3}{10} + \frac{1}{10}$ (i) $\frac{8}{9} - \frac{2}{9}$ (j) $\frac{5}{12} + \frac{3}{12}$

2 Simon spent $\frac{3}{10}$ of his holiday money on the first day of his holiday and
$\frac{1}{10}$ of his holiday money on the second day.

   (a) What fraction of his holiday money did Simon spend on the first two days?

   (b) What fraction did he have left for the remainder of his holiday?

3 Work these out.
Give each answer as a mixed (or whole) number in its simplest form.

   (a) $\frac{2}{3} + \frac{1}{3}$ (b) $\frac{4}{5} + \frac{2}{5}$ (c) $\frac{4}{9} + \frac{5}{9}$ (d) $\frac{5}{7} + \frac{6}{7}$ (e) $\frac{9}{10} + \frac{7}{10}$

4 Work these out, simplifying your answers where possible.

   (a) $\frac{1}{2} \times 10$ (b) $\frac{1}{4} \times 7$ (c) $\frac{2}{3} \times 4$ (d) $\frac{3}{4} \times 5$ (e) $\frac{4}{5} \times 6$

5 Aled uses $\frac{1}{3}$ pint of milk to make a milkshake.
How much milk does he need to make 10 milkshakes?

3 Reading scales

A Whole numbers
level 4

1 What number does each arrow point to?

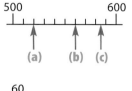 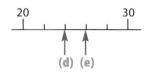 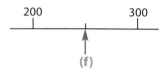

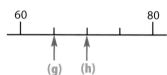  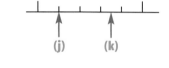

B Decimals
level 4

1 What number does each arrow point to?

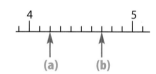 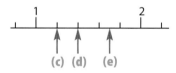 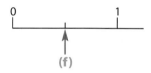

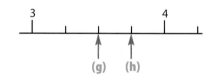 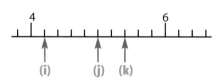

2 This graph shows the weight of a given length of a certain kind of copper tubing.

(a) What is the weight of a piece of this copper tubing with a length of 5 m?

(b) Estimate the weight of a piece of tubing that is 4.4 metres long.

(c) Estimate the length of a piece of this copper tubing that weighs

    (i) 4 kg   (ii) 2.5 kg

(d) Estimate the weight of a piece of tubing with a length of 2.5 m.

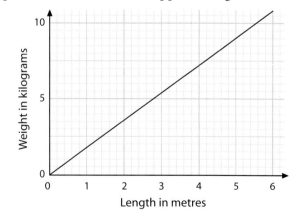

4 Arrow diagrams and equations

1 Copy and complete each of these arrow diagrams.

(a) (9) →÷ 3→ ( ) →+ 5→ ( )   (b) (7) →− 1→ ( ) →× 4→ ( )

(c) (2) →× 5→ ( ) →− 3→ ( )   (d) (12) →+ 3→ ( ) →÷ 3→ ( )

2 Copy and complete each of these arrow diagrams.

(a) ( ) →× 2→ ( ) →+ 7→ (13)   (b) ( ) →+ 1→ ( ) →× 7→ (14)

(c) ( ) →+ 10→ ( ) →÷ 3→ (5)   (d) ( ) →÷ 5→ ( ) →− 3→ (1)

3 Copy and complete each of these arrow diagrams.

(a) ( ) →+ 2→ ( ) →× 6→ ( ) →− 7→ (23)

(b) ( ) →− 7→ ( ) →÷ 4→ ( ) →+ 5→ (12)

B **Using letters**
C **Solving equations**

1 Match each arrow diagram with one of the equations underneath.

(a) ( ) →× 3→ ( ) →+ 5→ (17)   (b) ( ) →÷ 3→ ( ) →+ 5→ (17)

(c) ( ) →÷ 5→ ( ) →− 3→ (17)   (d) ( ) →× 5→ ( ) →− 3→ (17)

J $\dfrac{x}{5} - 3 = 17$ **K** $\dfrac{x}{3} + 5 = 17$ **L** $5x - 3 = 17$ **M** $3x + 5 = 17$

2 Draw an arrow diagram for each of these equations.
Then reverse the arrow diagram and solve the equation.

(a) $3x + 5 = 14$ (b) $10x + 6 = 46$ (c) $4x - 8 = 36$

(d) $2n - 4 = 10$ (e) $\dfrac{n}{4} + 4 = 7$ (f) $\dfrac{n}{5} + 3 = 5$

(g) $3y + 2 = 23$ (h) $\dfrac{y}{3} - 4 = 6$ (i) $\dfrac{y}{8} + 9 = 10$

(j) $5k - 9 = 16$ (k) $4k + 2 = 22$ (l) $\dfrac{k}{3} - 2 = 1$

3 Solve each equation.

(a) $5b - 7 = 8.5$ (b) $\dfrac{c}{9} - 1.3 = 4.7$ (c) $4n - 9.8 = 13$

D Number puzzles

1 Write down an equation for each of these number puzzles.
Solve your equation.

(a)
I think of a number.
I multiply by 5.
I add 6.
My answer is 51.
What was my number?

(b)
I think of a number.
I divide by 7.
I add 18.
My answer is 20.
What was my number?

(c)
I think of a number.
I multiply by 2.
I subtract 9.
My answer is 11.
What was my number?

(d)
I think of a number.
I multiply by 9.
I subtract 5.
My answer is 22.
What was my number?

(e)
I think of a number.
I divide by 2.
I subtract 14.
My answer is 1.
What was my number?

(f)
I think of a number.
I multiply by 4.
I add 18.
My answer is 30.
What was my number?

2 Write down a number puzzle for each of these equations.
Solve the equation.

(a) $4n - 2 = 18$ (b) $8n + 1 = 49$ (c) $\dfrac{n}{5} + 2 = 4.8$

5 Decimals

A One and two decimal places
B More than two decimal places

1 Decide whether each of these is true or false.

   (a) 4.2 is between 4.1 and 4.36   (b) 1.25 is between 1.3 and 1.39

2 In 1987, Stefka Kostadinova set a new women's world record in the high jump.
   She jumped over a bar that was 2.09 m above the ground.
   Which of these animals could walk under this bar without lowering its head?

   A A giraffe with a height of 4.2 m

   B A zebra with a height of 1.27 m

   C An elephant with a height of 2.4 m

3 Put each list of numbers in order, smallest first.

   (a) 1.3, 5, 3.6, 3.51, 1.29   (b) 0.46, 1, 0.8, 0.34, 0.09

4 Put each set of weights in order, smallest first.

   (a) 2.67 kg, 2.453 kg, 2.009 kg   (b) 5.4 kg, 5.329 kg, 5.24 kg

5 What number is halfway between

   (a) 2 and 3   (b) 8.2 and 8.3   (c) 1.82 and 1.83

C Rounding to the nearest whole number

1 Round these to the nearest centimetre.

   (a) 3.7 cm   (b) 9.4 cm   (c) 8.2 cm   (d) 19.8 cm   (e) 20.9 cm

2 Round these to the nearest kilometre.

   (a) 124.3 km   (b) 98.9 km   (c) 342.2 km   (d) 983.7 km   (e) 127.9 km

3 Round these to the nearest whole number.

   (a) 5.6   (b) 48.65   (c) 34.25   (d) 29.88   (e) 150.36

4 Round these to the nearest litre.

   (a) 6.54 litres   (b) 3.09 litres   (c) 13.43 litres   (d) 8.84 litres   (e) 10.75 litres

5 Round these to the nearest kilogram.

   (a) 7.812 kg   (b) 42.397 kg   (c) 915.071 kg   (d) 109.8 kg   (e) 0.691 kg

D Rounding to one decimal place
E Rounding to more than one decimal place

1 Round these numbers to one decimal place.
   (a) 15.63   (b) 7.893   (c) 10.745   (d) 1.405   (e) 3.96

2

A	E	C	K	R	H	S	B	D
4.0	4.1	4.2	4.3	4.4	4.5	4.6	4.7	4.8

Round each decimal below to one decimal place and find a letter for each one.
Rearrange each set of letters to spell an item of food.
   (a) 4.0937, 4.03, 4.1875, 4.3453
   (b) 4.477, 4.134, 4.059, 4.567, 4.235, 4.088
   (c) 4.392, 4.778, 4.7341, 4.079, 4.032

3 Round these numbers to two decimal places.
   (a) 4.9453   (b) 9.0673   (c) 24.189   (d) 4.2034

4 Round these amounts to the nearest penny.
   (a) £5.8351   (b) £20.949   (c) £6.079 83   (d) £32.499 23

5 Round these numbers to three decimal places.
   (a) 1.234 56   (b) 3.567 85   (c) 0.885 43   (d) 17.8999

F Multiplying and dividing by powers of ten

1 Calculate these.
   (a) 2.57 × 10   (b) 0.738 × 100   (c) 58.678 × 1000
   (d) 9.842 × 100   (e) 2.38 × 1000   (f) 1.7865 × 100

2 Calculate these.
   (a) 14.8 ÷ 10   (b) 369.32 ÷ 100   (c) 53 684.7 ÷ 1000
   (d) 9.7 ÷ 10   (e) 14 ÷ 100   (f) 1.9 ÷ 100

3 Calculate these.
   (a) 76.3 × 100   (b) 0.7861 × 1000   (c) 198.7 ÷ 100
   (d) 0.765 × 1000   (e) 10.769 ÷ 1000   (f) 76.93 × 1000

4 Find the missing number in each calculation.
   (a) ■ × 10 = 75.3   (b) 7321 ÷ ■ = 73.21   (c) 17.3 × ■ = 17 300

6 Angles, triangles and quadrilaterals

You need squared paper for section C.

A Review: angles round a point, on a line, in a triangle

The diagrams in this work are sketches.
That means they are not drawn accurately, so you must work out angles, not measure them.

Even so, if a line looks straight as it goes through a point where there are angles,
you should assume it is straight.

1 Calculate the angles marked with letters in these diagrams.

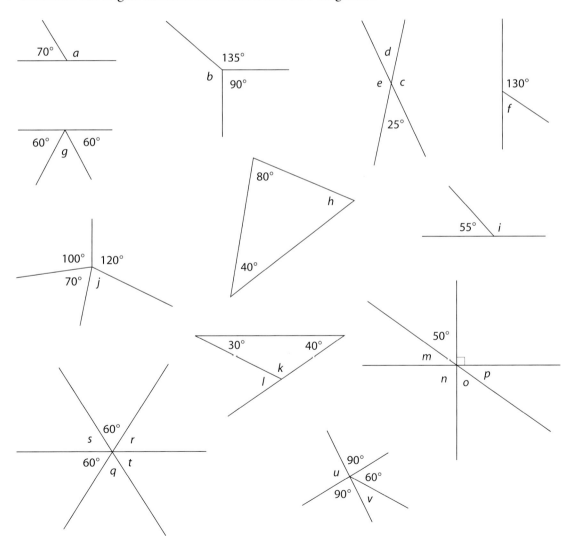

2 Find the angles marked by letters.
   Give a reason for each lettered angle that you find.

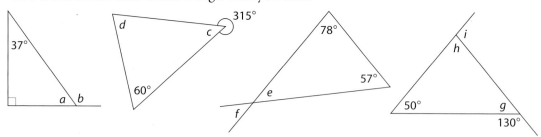

3 Find the angles marked by letters.

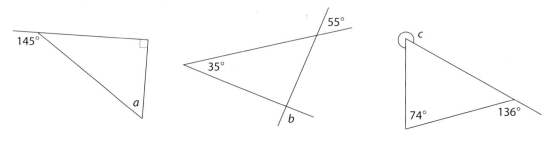

B Angles in an isosceles triangle

1 Find the angles marked by letters.

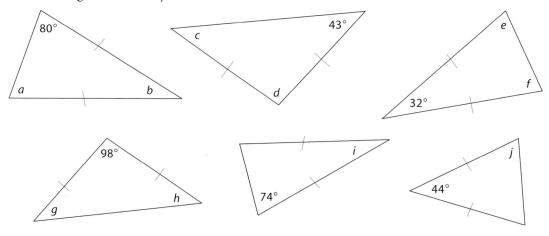

2 What special kind of triangle is this?
   Find the angles marked by letters.

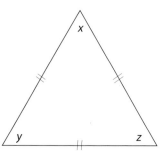

3 Find the angles marked by letters.

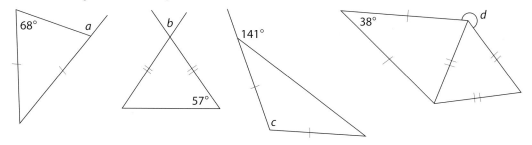

C Properties of special quadrilateral

1 On squared paper draw and label

  a rhombus

  a rectangle

  a kite

  a parallelogram

  Say which of these shapes have

  (a) two pairs of sides that are parallel and diagonals that are equal in length

  (b) two pairs of equal angles

  (c) only one pair of equal angles

  (d) two pairs of parallel sides, and diagonals that are not equal

  (e) diagonals that are perpendicular to each other but not equal,
       with one diagonal cutting the other in half

2 This is a sketch of the diagonals of a quadrilateral.

  (a) Draw the diagonals accurately.
       Join points ABCD to make the quadrilateral.

  (b) What type of quadrilateral have you drawn?

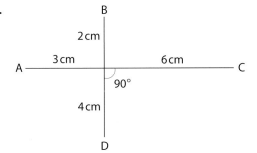

*3 A certain quadrilateral has just two vertices where the sides meet at 90°.

  (a) Give the names of two special quadrilateral that it could it be.

  (b) Does it have to be a special quadrilateral?
       If not, do a sketch showing what it could be like.

7 Experiments

A Specifying the problem and planning

Some students wanted to know whether pictures help people remember words.

Asad suggested this method.

- Make a list of 20 words with pictures, and the same list without pictures.
- Give 10 people a copy of the first list.
  After a minute, ask each person to write down the words they remember.
- Then give them the second list and do the same.
- Compare the number of words they remember.

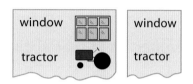

Brian suggested using the same method but with different words for the list without pictures.

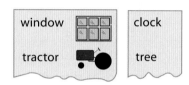

1 Which method, Asad's or Brian's, do you think is better? Why?

2 Describe briefly how the students could find out whether the pictures make more difference to boys than to girls.

B Processing and representing
C Interpreting and discussing

1 In an experiment, students in a class were asked to guess their teacher's age.
The answers they gave were

Girls	30 32 33 30 28 31 36 29 32 32 30 29 30 31 29
Boys	32 29 39 30 32 32 26 33 35 31 30 32 31 33 30 35 37

(a) Draw a dot plot showing the girls' guesses.

(b) Draw another dot plot, using the same scale, to show the boys' guesses.

(c) Find the median and range of the girls' guesses.

(d) Find the median and range of the boys' guesses.

(e) Which group, on average, thought the teacher was older, boys or girls?

(f) Whose guesses varied the most, boys' or girls'?

2 A group of students carried out an experiment where they tested their grip strength.
First they tested their grip using the hand they write with.
They then tested with their 'non-writing' hand.

The results were

Grip strength with writing hand (kg)	29 35 34 39 41 43 37 35 30 36
Grip strength with non-writing hand (kg)	28 26 48 27 32 36 24 28 31 27

(a) Make a copy of the scale on the right.
Use it to draw a dot plot for the students'
grip strength with their writing hand.

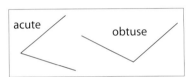

Writing hand grip strength (kg)

(b) Find the median of the students' grip strengths with their writing hand.

(c) Draw a dot plot for the students' grip strength with their non-writing hand.
Use a scale like the one before.

(d) Find the median of the students' grip strengths with their non-writing hand.

(e) Which hand, on average, had the stronger grip,
the writing hand or the non-writing hand?

3 A class was shown two angles, one acute and one obtuse.
The students were asked to estimate the size of each angle.
Here are the results, in degrees.

Acute angle	55 60 66 49 57 55 60 60 70 66
	62 59 54 48 55 51 63 68 62 57
Obtuse angle	120 123 115 118 123 135 130 100 115 127
	105 133 120 125 131 114 108 122 135 120

(a) Find the mean and range of each set of estimates.

(b) The actual sizes of the angles given to the class were

acute angle 56°   obtuse angle 113°

Write a short report comparing the estimates of each type of angle.

(c) One student thought it might be easier to estimate an angle
if one 'arm' were horizontal, like this: and not this:

The class were given two acute angles, one 'horizontal' and one not.
Here is a summary of the estimates.

Angle	Mean estimate	Range of estimates	Actual size
'Horizontal'	36.2°	4.0°	37°
'Non-horizontal'	61.8°	7.0°	64°

Do the results support what the student thought? Explain your answer.

8 Multiples, factors and primes

A Multiples

level 4

1 Which numbers in this list are multiples of 7?

42, 24, 14, 17, 18, 700, 71, 49

2 Which numbers in this list are multiples of 3?

23, 12, 9, 15, 31, 300, 28, 24

3 Write down six different multiples of 6 that are less than 64.

4 Write down six different multiples of 9 that are less than 100.

5 Write down all the multiples of 8 that lie between 30 and 50.

6 (a) Which numbers in the loop are multiples of

(i) 7   (ii) 2

(iii) 11   (iv) 5

(v) 4   (vi) 5 **and** 4

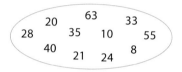

(b) List all the numbers in the loop that are even multiples of 5.

(c) Which numbers in the loop are odd multiples of 3?

B Factors

level 4

1 One number in this list is not a factor of 12. Which is it?

2, 3, 4, 5, 6, 12

2 Two numbers in this list are not factors of 18. Which are they?

2, 3, 4, 6, 8, 9

3 List all the factors of

(a) 8   (b) 12   (c) 30   (d) 16   (e) 13

4 Show how you can fit the numbers 3, 4, 5 and 8 into this grid, one number in each box.

	is a factor of 24	is a factor of 20
is a factor of 40		
is a factor of 12		

5 List all the factors of 72.

C Multiples and factors

1 Decide which of these statements are true and which are false.

(a) 3 is a factor of 12.

(b) 9 is a multiple of 3.

(c) 15 is a factor of 5.

(d) 5 is a factor of 25.

(e) 18 is a multiple of 6.

(f) 16 is a factor of 4.

2 Which word, either 'factor' or 'multiple', should go in each statement?

(a) 4 is a ……………… of 24.

(b) 7 is a ……………… of 28.

(c) 15 is a ……………… of 3.

(d) 9 is a ……………… of 27.

(e) 21 is a ……………… of 3.

(f) 15 is a ……………… of 45.

3 Write down a number from the loop to complete each statement.

(a) ▓ is a factor of 12.

(b) ▓ is a multiple of 5.

(c) 9 is a factor of ▓.

(d) ▓ is a multiple of 24.

27   17
40   48   6

D Common multiples and factors

1 Which of these are common multiples of 3 and 5?

9, 10, 15, 20, 30, 50, 90

2 Which of these are common factors of 12 and 32?

1, 2, 4, 5, 6, 8, 9, 10

3 List five different common multiples of 4 and 10.

4 List all the common factors of

(a) 12 and 18

(b) 10 and 15

(c) 8 and 20

5 Give the lowest common multiple of the following pairs of numbers.

(a) 3 and 4

(b) 5 and 7

(c) 12 and 20

6 Give the highest common factor of the following pairs of numbers.

(a) 15 and 25

(b) 24 and 36

(c) 42 and 48

7 What is the highest common factor of 31 and 32?

*8 Jed has 20p.
Zak has 45p.

They both buy some toffees.
They both spend all their money.

What is the maximum cost of a toffee?

E Prime numbers

1 List all the prime numbers between 20 and 30.

2 Four of the numbers in the loop are **not** prime.
Which are they?

3 Which of the numbers below are prime?

12, 7, 48, 31, 5, 17

4 List all the prime numbers between 40 and 50.

5 How can you tell that no numbers below are prime?

4, 56, 24, 128, 16, 34

6 Use the clues to find the numbers.

(a)
| A prime number |
| Larger than 35 |
| Smaller than 40 |

(b)
| A prime number |
| Larger than 8 |
| Smaller than 15 |
| A factor of 33 |

(c)
| A prime number with two digits |
| Digits add to make 11 |
| Larger than 70 |

F Products of prime factors

1 Write 30 as a product of prime factors.

2 For each number below, make a factor tree and write the number as a product of primes.

(a) 16   (b) 24   (c) 100   (d) 75   (e) 600

3 (a) (i) Write 77 as a product of primes.

(ii) Write 84 as a product of primes.

(b) Find the highest common factor of 77 and 84.

(c) Which of these gives the lowest common multiple of 77 and 84?

A $2 \times 3 \times 7 \times 11$ B $2 \times 2 \times 3 \times 7 \times 11$ C $2 \times 2 \times 3 \times 7 \times 7 \times 11$

4 Find the highest common factor of each pair of numbers by first writing each number as a product of prime factors.

(a) 21 and 35   (b) 42 and 30   (c) 44 and 132

5 Find the lowest common multiple of each pair of numbers by first writing each number as a product of prime factors.

(a) 26 and 39   (b) 54 and 99   (c) 24 and 108

Mixed practice 1

You need squared paper.

1 Look at the numbers in this box.

2	4	12	15
16	24	25	27

  (a) Which of the numbers are factors of 12?

  (b) Which of the numbers are multiples of 6?

  (c) Which of the numbers is prime?

2 Each child at a party eats $\frac{1}{3}$ of a pizza.
How many pizzas do 12 children at this party eat?

3 Draw a grid going from $^-4$ to 4 on both axes.

  (a) Plot the points $(3, 1)$, $(^-3, 3)$, and $(2, ^-2)$.

  (b) (i) Add another point to make a rectangle.

     (ii) What are the coordinates of this point?

  (c) Show all the lines of symmetry on this rectangle.

4 How many sides has a pentagon?

5 Draw an arrow diagram for each of these equations.
Reverse each diagram to solve the equation. Check your answers work.

  (a) $3x + 2 = 26$ (b) $4w - 5 = 23$ (c) $\frac{k}{5} + 3 = 6$

6 Work out the size of each of the angles marked with a letter.

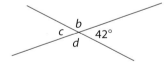
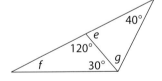

7 (a) Salvador has 20 rabbits. 12 of them are male.
What fraction of Salvador's rabbits are male?
Write the fraction in its simplest form.

  (b) Salvador also has 24 piglets.
$\frac{3}{8}$ of them are less than 6 months old.
How many of his piglets are less than 6 months old?

8 A group of year 10 students were asked how many hours they spent
doing their homework last week.

The results were: 12, 10, 8, 4, 3, 8, 9, 5, 8, 7, 11, 5

  (a) Work out the range of times spent doing homework.

  (b) Work out the median time spent.

  (c) Calculate the mean time.

9 This graph can be used to convert between inches and centimetres.

   (a) Use the graph to convert each of these to centimetres.

       (i)   3 inches

       (ii) 1.5 inches

       (iii) 1 inch

   (b) Use the graph to convert each of these to inches.

       (i)   5 centimetres

       (ii) 6.4 centimetres

       (iii) 3.5 centimetres

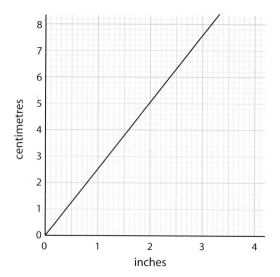

10 (a) Find the lowest common multiple of 6 and 21.

   (b) Find the highest common factor of 36 and 27.

11 Round these quantities.

   (a) 15.37 kg to the nearest kilogram   (b) 12.2375 to two decimal places

   (c) 0.876 65 to three decimal places

12 This design has rotation symmetry of order 3.

   (a) What is the special name for each yellow triangle?

   (b) How many lines of symmetry has the design?

   (c) What is the special name for the blue triangle?

   (d) Find the size of each angle marked with a letter.

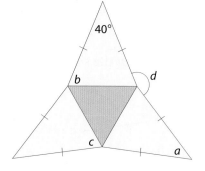

13 Work these out.

   (a) 0.25×10 (b) 7.4×100 (c) $6924 \div 1000$ (d) $1.4 \div 100$

14 Work out $\frac{3}{4} \times 5$ and write the answer as a mixed number.

15 Put each of these sets of numbers in order, smallest first.

   (a) 5.5, 5.25, 5.03, 5.15, 5.52   (b) 1, 0.082, 0.25, 0.05, 0.5, 0.853

16 A quadrilateral has rotation symmetry of order 2.
   Its diagonals are perpendicular to each other.
   What is the special name for this quadrilateral?

17 Write 56 as a product of prime factors.

9 Working with formulas 1

1 Work out the value of each of these when $n = 5$.

(a) $n + 3$ (b) $n - 1$ (c) $3n$ (d) $n - 5$

2 Work out the value of each of these when $a = 3$.

(a) $2a - 1$ (b) $2(a - 1)$ (c) $4a + 3$ (d) $4(a + 3)$

B Arranging tables and chairs

1 Bob's Brasserie uses rectangular tables for large groups of people.
They set out these tables with chairs in long rows like this.

With three of these tables, they would need 20 chairs.

(a) How many chairs do they need for 2 of these tables arranged like this?

(b) How many do they need for 5 tables?

(c) How many do they need for 100 tables?

(d) Copy and complete this table.

Number of tables	1	2	3	4	5	6	10	100
Number of chairs			20					

(e) Here are some rules connecting the number of tables and the number of chairs.
Which of the rules is correct?

number of chairs = number of tables + 6	number of chairs = number of tables × 6 + 2
number of chairs = number of tables × 8	number of chairs = number of tables × 2 + 6

(f) Suppose c stands for the number of chairs and t stands for the number of tables.
Which of these formulas is correct?

$c = 8t$ $c = 2(t + 3)$ $c = 6t + 2$ $c = t + 6$

c Designing pendants

1 Jason uses small plastic blocks to make pendant designs.

This is his Basic design.

Size 1   Size 2   Size 3

(a) How many blocks does Jason use in a size 4 Basic design?

(b) How many blocks are used in a size 10 Basic design?

(c) If Jason made a size 20 Basic design, how many blocks would he need?

(d) How can you work out the number of blocks needed when you know the size number?

(e) Choose one of the expressions below to complete this sentence.

> If the size number of a Basic design is n then the number of blocks in it is …

| $3n$ | $2(n + 1)$ | $2n + 1$ | $4n + 2$ | $n + 2$ |

2 This is Jason's Petal design.
On the left is a size 2; on the right is a size 4.

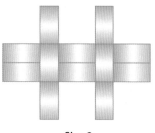   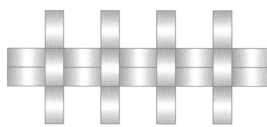

Size 2   Size 4

(a) Which of these expressions tells you the number of blocks in a size n Petal design?

| $7n$ | $5n + 2$ | $5n + 4$ | $2n + 2$ | $5(n + 2)$ |

(b) How many blocks would Jason need for a size 8 Petal design?

D Equations and arrow diagrams

1 Lisa fixes together wooden posts to build fences.
  A size n Tribar fence has $4n + 1$ posts in it.

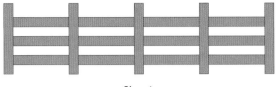

Size 4

(a) Check that the expression is correct for the size 4 fence above.

(b) One size of Tribar fence has 61 posts in it.
   Copy and complete this working to find out what size Tribar fence it is.

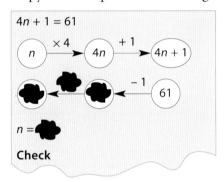

2 A size n Propped fence is made from
  $4n + 3$ posts.

  One Propped fence is made from 95 posts.
  Work out what size it is.
  Show all your working and check your answer.

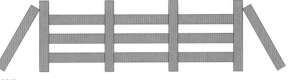

Size 3

3 Below are three sizes of Lisa's Hurdle fence.

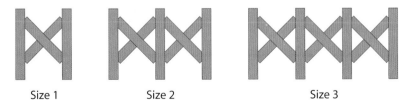

Size 1   Size 2   Size 3

(a) Which of these expressions tells you
   the number of posts in a size n Hurdle fence?

   | $4n$ | $4n + 3$ | $3n + 1$ |

   | $n + 1$ | $n + 3$ |

(b) Lisa makes a Hurdle fence with 82 posts.
   Work out what size it is.

10 Representing 3-D objects

You need triangular dotty paper and centimetre squared paper for section AB.

A The Soma cube
B Plan and elevations

1 Here are two Soma cube pieces drawn on triangular dotty paper.

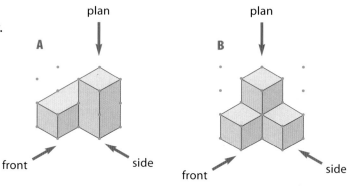

(a) The plan views for these Soma cube pieces are shown here.
Which is the plan view for piece A?

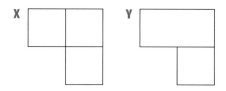

(b) Draw the front view for piece A.

(c) Draw the side view for piece B.

2 This shape is made from five centimetre cubes.

(a) Draw the shape on triangular dotty paper.

(b) Draw full-size on centimetre squared paper
   (i) a plan view   (ii) a front view
   (iii) a side view

3 This diagram shows a solid object with some measurements.
Draw full-size on centimetre squared paper

(a) a plan view

(b) a front view

(c) a side view

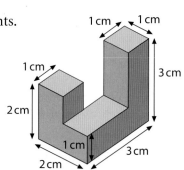

1 This is a triangular prism.

Which two of these could be nets of this prism?

A 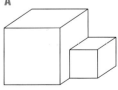   **B**    **C** 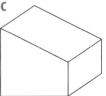   **D**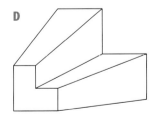

2 This is a matchbox tray with its measurements.
Draw an accurate net of the tray.

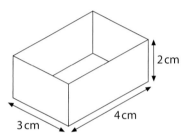

3 This is a triangular prism.
The ends of the prism are right-angled triangles.
Draw an accurate full-size net of this prism.

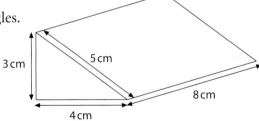

4 **A**   **B**   **C**   **D**

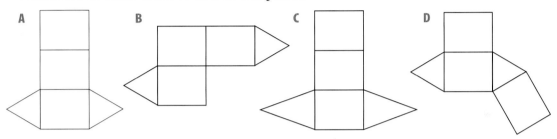

One of the objects above is a prism.

(a) Which one is it?

(b) Sketch its cross-section.

E Reflection symmetry

1 This shape is made from six cubes.
  Which of the shapes below is
  a mirror image of this shape?

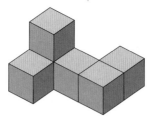

A 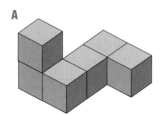   **B** 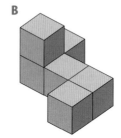   **C**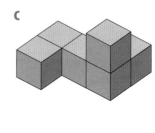

2 Each of these shapes is made from six cubes.
  How many planes of symmetry does each shape have?

(a) 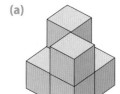   **(b)** 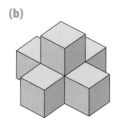   **(c)**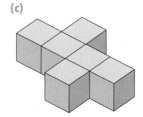

3 How many planes of symmetry does each of these shapes have?

(a)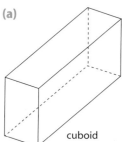

cuboid

(b)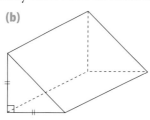

isosceles triangle prism

(c)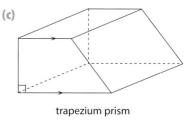

trapezium prism

4 This solid is a prism made from cubes.
  How many planes of symmetry does it have?

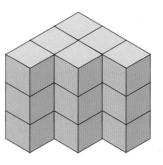

11 Written calculation 1

A Adding and subtracting whole numbers and decimals

1 Work these out.

(a) 270 + 128   (b) 682 − 302   (c) 207 + 24   (d) 571 − 95   (e) 708 + 295

2 Work these out.

(a) 3.42 − 2.31   (b) 4.03 + 2.49   (c) 3.7 + 1.94   (d) 8.59 − 1.4   (e) 7.5 − 1.36

3 Josh is 1.4 m tall. Darnell is 1.37 m tall.
Who is taller, and by how much?

4 Whose shopping is heavier, Jo's or David's? By how much?

Jo

David

0.5 kg
2.5 kg
1.76 kg
3.15 kg

0.35 kg
2.65 kg
1.08 kg
3.25 kg

B Multiplying whole numbers

1

0	1	2	3	4	5	6	7	8	9
P	A	T	C	H	W	O	R	K	S

Work out the multiplications below.
Use the code above to make a word for each answer.

(a) 6 × 613   (b) 314 × 7   (c) 1852 × 5

(d) 3155 × 3   (e) 4 × 8543   (f) 12 553 × 3

2 (a) A mile is 1760 yards. There are 3 feet in a yard. How many feet are there in a mile?

(b) A stone is 14 pounds. How many pounds are there in 8 stones?

(c) There are 8 pints in a gallon. How many pints is 24 gallons?

3 Tickets for a concert cost £6 each.
How much money is collected from the sale of 195 tickets?

C Multiplying decimals

1 Work these out.

    (a) 2.9×3 (b) 1.45×5 (c) 2.14×3 (d) 4.28×4 (e) 6.29×6

2 How much will it cost to buy 6 cards at £1.40 each?

3 (a) One kilogram is about 2.2 pounds.
      How many pounds does a 7 kg bag of potatoes weigh?

    (b) A litre is about 1.75 pints. How many pints does a 5 litre container hold?

4 Four friends go out bowling. One game of bowling costs £4.95.
   How much do the four friends pay altogether?

5 A bottle contains 0.75 litres of apple juice.
   How much juice do 6 of these bottles contain?

D Dividing whole numbers

1 Work these out.

    (a) $189 \div 3$ (b) $924 \div 6$ (c) $2528 \div 8$ (d) $1015 \div 7$ (e) $3807 \div 9$

2 Find three pairs of divisions that give the same answer.
   Which division is the odd one out?

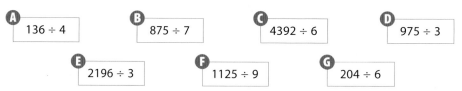

3 Oranges are sold in bags of 5.

    (a) How many bags can be filled from 467 oranges?

    (b) How many oranges will be left over?

4 Each table in a school dining room seats 8 people.

    (a) How many tables will be needed for 675 people?

    (b) How many empty seats will there be?

5 A car transporter can carry 7 cars.
   How many transporter loads will be needed to move 1580 cars?

6 Richard is packing muffins into boxes of 6.
   He has 140 muffins.
   How many boxes can he fill?

E Dividing decimals

1 Work these out.

   (a) 8.6 ÷ 2   (b) 3.6 ÷ 4   (c) 1.25 ÷ 5   (d) 12.35 ÷ 5   (e) 15.3 ÷ 9

   (f) 6.3 ÷ 2   (g) 2.5 ÷ 2   (h) 6.4 ÷ 5   (i) 8.6 ÷ 4   (j) 22.8 ÷ 8

2 A plank of wood measuring 3.45 m is cut into 5 equal length pieces.
How long is each piece?

3 15 kg from a sack of flour is divided into 4 equal bags.
How much flour is in each bag?

4

A	C	E	G	H	L	P	R	Y
1.5	1.25	0.2	0.5	1.7	0.3	0.4	2.5	0.82

Find the answers to these questions. Then use the code to get a letter for each answer.
Rearrange each set of letters to spell a fruit.

(a)	(b)	(c)	(d)
4.1 ÷ 5	2.4 ÷ 6	10 ÷ 8	0.8 ÷ 2
10 ÷ 4	2.7 ÷ 9	8.5 ÷ 5	7.5 ÷ 5
5.1 ÷ 3	0.8 ÷ 4	3 ÷ 2	5 ÷ 2
2.5 ÷ 2	2 ÷ 5	1.6 ÷ 4	4 ÷ 8
1.6 ÷ 8	6 ÷ 4	1 ÷ 5	1.2 ÷ 6
7.5 ÷ 3			

F Mixed questions

1 Tracy was making up some squash in a 3 litre container.
She poured in 0.45 litres of orange, and then filled the container with water.
How much water did she add?

2 A one pound coin has a diameter of 2.2 cm.
How long will a line of 8 one pound coins be?

3 The perimeter of a rectangle is the distance all the way round it.
This rectangle has a perimeter 3.4 m.
It is 0.8 m wide.
What is its length?

    0.8 m

4 Maryam buys 2 tins of soup at 49p each, a loaf of bread at 85p and
a piece of cheese at £2.40.
She pays with a £10 note.
How much change should she get?

5 Jan takes 8 minutes to make a birthday card.
At this rate, how many of these birthday cards can she make in one hour?

12 Frequency

You need squared paper for section D.

A Stem-and-leaf tables
B Median and range

1 This data shows the number of visitors to an exhibition each day in February.

24	36	41	17	25	36	22	13	49	34	16	23	19	25
32	47	37	15	27	29	31	28	47	39	16	21	30	19

(a) Record the data in a stem-and-leaf table using this stem.
Rewrite the table putting the leaves in order.

(b) What was the highest number of visitors?

(c) Find the median number of visitors.

(d) Work out the range of the number of visitors.

1	
2	4
3	6
4	
5	

Stem: 10 people

2 This table shows the number of visitors to the exhibition in March.

1	1 2 2 2 4 5 6 7 7 8 8
2	2 3 4 4 5 6 6 6 7 9 9
3	0 2 2 3 6 7
4	1 4
5	2

Stem: 10 people

(a) On how many days were there fewer than 25 visitors?

(b) Find the median number of visitors in March.

(c) Find the range of the number of visitors in March.

3 Class 11S sell raffle tickets for charity.
The table shows the number of tickets
sold by each student.

15	27	34	41	20	36	14	7	15	26
31	45	28	14	8	19	27	36	21	30
40	49	22	7	5	11	35	25	21	19

(a) Make an ordered stem-and-leaf table for this data
using the stem shown.

(b) What was the median number of tickets sold?

(c) What was the range of the number of tickets?

(d) Any student selling more than 35 tickets won a prize.
How many students won a prize?

0	
1	
2	
3	
4	

Stem: 10 tickets

c Comparisons

1 James is comparing two different types of tomato plant.
He counts the number of tomatoes he picks from each plant.
This table shows the results for the two types of plant.

Many Maker		Tasty Toms
6 3	**2**	1
7 4 2	**3**	4 5
8 5 5 3	**4**	6 8 8
4 4 2	**5**	3 7 9
3	**6**	8

Stem: 10 tomatoes

(a) Find the median and range of the number of tomatoes from Many Maker plants.

(b) Find the median and range of tomatoes from Tasty Toms plants.

(c) Which type of plant gave James more tomatoes on average?
Explain how you know.

2 Marie counts the number of aubergines growing on two types of plant.
This table shows the number of aubergines growing on the two types of plant.

Black Beauty		Long Purple
9 6	**0**	7 8 8
8 8 3 1 1	**1**	0 1 2 6 7
9 9 7 4	**2**	1 3 6 8
4 0	**3**	

Stem: 10 aubergines

(a) Find the median and range of the number of aubergines for each type of plant.

(b) Which type of plant gave Marie more aubergines on average?

D Grouping

1 The graph shows the ages of people who visited Metro Movies DVD hire shop one Tuesday.

(a) How many people aged 40–59 visited Metro Movies on Tuesday?

(b) How many people aged under 40 visited Metro Movies on Tuesday?

(c) What was the modal age group for Tuesday?

(d) How many people in total visited Metro Movies on Tuesday?

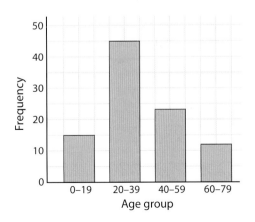

2 This table shows the ages of people who visited
  Metro Movies on the previous Saturday.

Age group	Frequency
0–19	25
20–39	44
40–59	51
60–79	10

  (a) Use the table to draw a bar chart of the people
      visiting Metro Movies on Saturday.

  (b) (i)   How many people in total visited Metro Movies
            on Saturday?

      (ii) How many more people visited Metro Movies on Saturday than Tuesday?

      (iii) Why do you think the number of visitors is so different on the two days?

  (c) Give two differences between the people who went to Metro Movies on
      Tuesday and those who went on Saturday.

3 The shop records the number of DVDs
  rented by a sample of its customers
  over a period of 3 months.

12	20	6	13	25	37	47	15	55	29	11	8	42
18	24	30	26	19	2	25	15	38	29	46	3	12
31	23	12	19	51	28	22	11	33	10	20	16	18

  (a) Record this data in a frequency table
      like the one shown here.

Number of DVDs	Tally	Frequency
0–9		
10–19		

  (b) Use your table to draw a bar chart of the number of DVDs
      rented by these customers.

E Mean

1 Bradley and George are practising throwing the discus.
  Their coach records the lengths of their throws.

| Bradley | 23.02 m | 22.43 m | 21.78 m | 19.85 m | 20.89 m | 21.42 m | 24.61 m | 22.48 m |
| George | 20.49 m | 21.07 m | 21.23 m | 26.84 m | 20.21 m | 19.64 m | 21.38 m | 22.80 m |

  (a) Work out the mean and range of Bradley's lengths.

  (b) Work out the mean and range of George's lengths.

  (c) Who should the coach pick for the team?
      Give reasons for your decision.

2 Paige surveyed some people leaving a local
  supermarket to find out how many
  carrier bags they had used.

Number of bags	Number of people
0	5
1	13
2	10
3	21
4	26
5	14
6	9

  (a) How many people had used 5 bags?

  (b) How many people were surveyed?

  (c) Work out the mean number of bags used.

  (d) What was the modal number of bags used?

13 Fractions, decimals and percentages

A Fractions and percentages

1 (a) What fraction of this shape is shaded?

(b) Write this fraction as a percentage.

2 Which is bigger, $\frac{3}{4}$ or 80%?
Explain how you know.

3 Sort these into four matching pairs.

| 50% | | 60% | | $\frac{3}{5}$ | | $\frac{1}{5}$ |

| | 20% | | 25% | | $\frac{1}{4}$ | | $\frac{1}{2}$ |

4 Write these in order of size, starting with the smallest.

70% $\frac{1}{2}$ 40% $\frac{3}{5}$ 30% $\frac{8}{10}$

B Decimals and percentages

1 Write each of these decimals as a percentage.

(a) 0.1   (b) 0.35   (c) 0.9   (d) 0.55

2 Write each of these percentages as a decimal.

(a) 20%   (b) 75%   (c) 65%   (d) 80%

3 Diane says that 0.4 is the same as 4%.
Explain why she is wrong.

4 Write each of these lists in order of size, starting with the smallest.

(a) 0.4   60%   0.2   0.65   25%   (b) 90%   0.45   55%   30%   0.7

C Fractions and decimals

1 (a) What fraction of this shape is shaded?

(b) Write this fraction as a decimal.

2 Which is smaller, 0.4 or $\frac{1}{4}$? Explain your answer.

3 Which is larger, 0.75 or $\frac{7}{10}$? Explain your answer.

4 Change each fraction to a decimal using division.

(a) $\frac{1}{5}$ (b) $\frac{2}{5}$ (c) $\frac{5}{8}$ (d) $\frac{7}{8}$

5 Write each of these lists in order of size, starting with the smallest.

(a) $\frac{3}{5}$ 0.8 $\frac{3}{10}$ 0.1 $\frac{3}{4}$ (b) 0.4 $\frac{9}{10}$ $\frac{1}{2}$ 0.25 $\frac{4}{5}$

D Thirds
E Converting between fractions, decimals and percentages

1 Copy and complete this table.

Fraction	Decimal	Percentage
$\frac{81}{100}$		
	0.67	
		74%
	0.01	
$\frac{9}{100}$		
		6%

2 Write each of these percentages as a fraction in its lowest terms.

(a) 30%   (b) 75%   (c) 80%   (d) 5%   (e) 24%

3 Which is smaller, $\frac{1}{3}$ or 30%? Explain how you know.

4 Which is larger, $\frac{2}{3}$ or 0.6? Explain how you know.

5 Write each of these lists in order of size, smallest first.

(a) 0.27 $\frac{1}{4}$ $\frac{1}{5}$ 30%   0.4   (b) 0.8 $\frac{3}{4}$ $\frac{3}{5}$ 0.67 $\frac{9}{10}$

(c) 25% $\frac{1}{5}$ $\frac{1}{2}$ 0.06   0.1   (d) $\frac{4}{5}$ 0.9 $\frac{2}{3}$ 0.85   60%

6 Lee and James entered a fun run.
Lee ran for 70% of the race. James ran for $\frac{3}{5}$ of the race.
Who ran further? Explain how you decide.

7 Kira was late to school on 6% of the days one term.
Max was late on $\frac{1}{10}$ of the days.
Who was late more often? Explain how you decide.

*8 In a college, 45% of the students arrive using public transport.
$\frac{1}{4}$ of the students walk or cycle.
The rest of the students arrive by car.
What percentage of the students arrive by car?

14 Area of a parallelogram

You need centimetre squared paper in section A.

A Changing a parallelogram into a rectangle

1 These parallelograms are drawn on centimetre squared paper
Find the area of each one. Use the correct units in each answer.

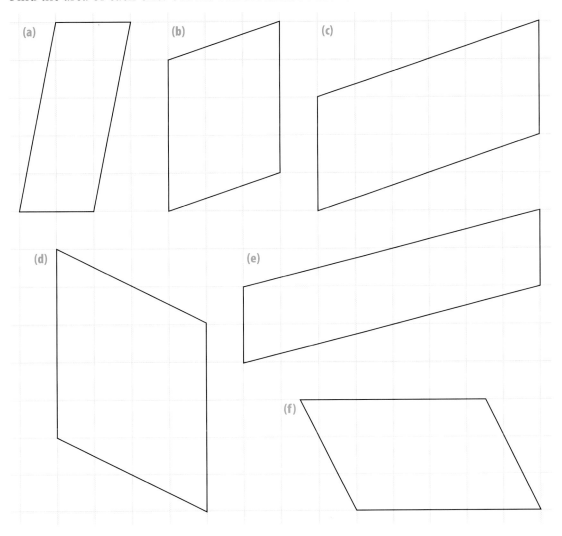

(a)

(b)

(c)

(d)

(e)

(f)

2 On centimetre squared paper, draw
  (a) three different parallelograms each with an area of $12\,cm^2$
  (b) three different parallelograms each with an area of $15\,cm^2$

B Using the formula

1 Find the areas of these parallelograms by measuring the base and height shown.
Use the correct units.

(a)

(b)

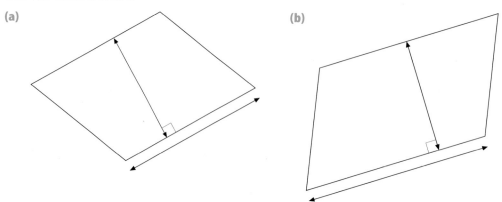

2 Find the areas of the parallelograms sketched here.

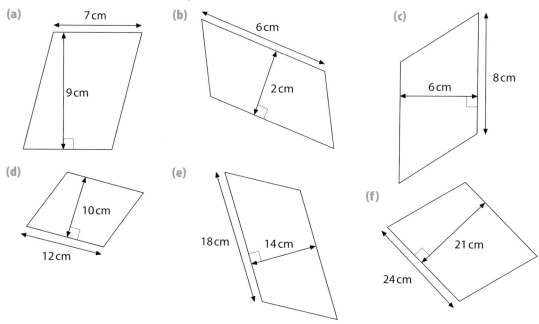

(a) 7 cm, 9 cm

(b) 6 cm, 2 cm

(c) 6 cm, 8 cm

(d) 10 cm, 12 cm

(e) 18 cm, 14 cm

(f) 21 cm, 24 cm

3 Find the areas of these 'overhanging' parallelograms.

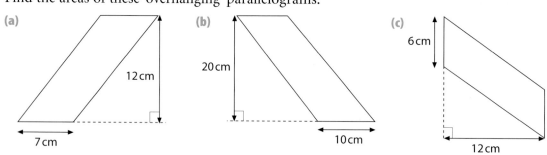

(a) 12 cm, 7 cm

(b) 20 cm, 10 cm

(c) 6 cm, 12 cm

15 Negative numbers

A Temperature changes

1 Write each list of temperatures in order, lowest first.

   (a) ⁻7°C   3°C   ⁻2°C   0°C   5°C   (b) ⁻1°C   2.5°C   ⁻7.5°C   ⁻4°C   5°C

2 At 5 a.m. the temperature was ⁻6°C.
  By 9 a.m. the temperature had risen by 10 degrees.
  What was the temperature at 9 a.m.?

3 Tara measures the temperature in her fridge as 4°C.
  She measures the temperature in her freezer as ⁻18°C.
  How much colder is it in the freezer than in the fridge?

4 Copy and complete this table.

Start temperature	Change	End temperature
1°C	rise 5 degrees	6°C
4°C	fall 7 degrees	
⁻2°C		3°C
	rise 3 degrees	0°C
⁻5°C		⁻1°C
⁻6°C	fall 4 degrees	

B Adding negative numbers

1 Work these out.

   (a) 3 + ⁻1   (b) 7 + ⁻2   (c) ⁻4 + ⁻2   (d) 10 + ⁻3   (e) ⁻1 + 9
   (f) ⁻6 + ⁻2   (g) ⁻3 + ⁻7   (h) ⁻2 + 11   (i) ⁻8 + ⁻4   (j) 3 + ⁻9

2 From the numbers in the loop,
  find two numbers that add up to   ⁻4   5
                                        ⁻6   2

   (a) ⁻10   (b) ⁻1   (c) 1   (d) ⁻4   (e) ⁻2

3 Work these out.

   (a) 10 + ⁻3 + ⁻2   (b) ⁻2 + ⁻3 + ⁻7   (c) 6 − 3 − 5   (d) ⁻8 + 3 + ⁻2

4 Find the missing number in each calculation.

   (a) ⁻3 + ■ = ⁻2   (b) ■ + ⁻1 = ⁻5   (c) ■ + 2 = ⁻6   (d) 4 + ■ = ⁻3

C Subtracting a negative number

1 Work these out.

(a) $6 - {}^-2$ (b) $5 - {}^-1$ (c) $10 - {}^-3$ (d) $4 - {}^-2$ (e) $8 - {}^-6$

(f) ${}^-4 - {}^-1$ (g) ${}^-2 - {}^-5$ (h) ${}^-3 - {}^-8$ (i) $3 - {}^-4$ (j) $1 - {}^-1$

2 Find three pairs that give the same answer.

| ${}^-5 + {}^-3$ | $3 - 7$ | ${}^-4 - {}^-2$ | ${}^-10 - {}^-2$ | $2 - 4$ | ${}^-1 + {}^-3$ |

3 Work these out.

(a) ${}^-3 + 9$ (b) ${}^-3 - 9$ (c) ${}^-3 + {}^-9$ (d) ${}^-3 - {}^-9$

(e) ${}^-2 + {}^-7$ (f) ${}^-2 - {}^-7$ (g) $2 - 7$ (h) $2 - {}^-7$

(i) $4 - 8$ (j) ${}^-4 - 8$ (k) ${}^-4 - {}^-8$ (l) $4 - {}^-8$

4 Use the numbers in the loop
to complete these calculations.

${}^-5 \quad {}^-3 \quad 3 \quad 5$

(a) ▦ + ▦ = ${}^-8$ (b) ▦ − ▦ = ${}^-2$ (c) ▦ + ▦ = ${}^-2$ (d) ▦ − ▦ = 8

D Multiplying a negative by a positive number

1 Work these out.

(a) ${}^-3 \times 5$ (b) ${}^-4 \times 7$ (c) ${}^-2 \times 8$ (d) $4 \times {}^-3$ (e) $5 \times {}^-5$

(f) $10 \times {}^-3$ (g) ${}^-4 \times 25$ (h) ${}^-3 \times 16$ (i) $6 \times {}^-20$ (j) ${}^-3 \times 15$

2

A	E	I	L	N	P	R	S	T	U	Y
${}^-20$	${}^-5$	1	${}^-8$	${}^-3$	${}^-18$	${}^-6$	5	${}^-15$	3	${}^-2$

Work out the answers to the questions below.
Use the code to change them to letters.
Rearrange the letters to make countries.

(a) $6 \times {}^-3$
     $1 - {}^-2$
     ${}^-2 \times 3$
     $1 - 6$

(b) ${}^-5 - {}^-2$
     $3 + {}^-2$
     ${}^-2 + 7$
     $2 \times {}^-9$
     ${}^-5 \times 4$

(c) ${}^-8 - {}^-6$
     $2 \times {}^-10$
     ${}^-4 \times 2$
     ${}^-8 - 7$
     ${}^-3 - {}^-4$

(d) $3 - {}^-2$
     $0 - {}^-3$
     $3 \times {}^-2$
     ${}^-8 + 9$
     ${}^-12 + {}^-8$
     $8 + {}^-3$

*3 Solve this number puzzle.

> I think of two numbers.
> The two numbers multiply to give ${}^-8$.
> The two numbers add to give 2.
> What could the two numbers be?

16 Metric units

A Using metric units

1 Without using a ruler, estimate
   (a) the width of your hand
   (b) the thickness of this book
   (c) the length of your little finger
   (d) the length of your arm from wrist to elbow

2 For each statement, what is the missing metric unit of length, millimetres, centimetres, metres or kilometres?
   (a) The length of my hand is 17 ....
   (b) The thickness of the book I am reading is 24 ....
   (c) The distance from London to New York is 5585 ....
   (d) The height of my bedroom is 2.5 ....

3 What metric unit of length would you use to measure
   (a) the width of a carpet
   (b) the distance from Bristol to Newcastle
   (c) the height of a can
   (d) the width of a spider

4 What unit would you use, grams or kilograms, to estimate the weight of
   (a) a pig
   (b) a sparrow
   (c) a mouse

5 For this statement, what is the missing metric unit of volume, millilitres or litres?
   The capacity of the bath is 80 ....

6 What is the missing metric unit in each statement?
   (a) The weight of a lemon is 120 ....
   (b) A golden eagle has a wingspan of more than 2 ....
   (c) The volume of shampoo in a bottle is 250 ....
   (d) The length of the World's longest road tunnel is 16.3 ....
   (e) The weight of a bull African elephant is 5000 ....
   (f) An adult man has about 5 .... of blood in his body.

7 Write down the metric unit you would use to measure
   (a) the circumference of a person's head
   (b) the amount of water in a paddling pool
   (c) the height of a waterfall
   (d) a tablespoon of oil
   (e) the weight of a baby

B Converting between metric units

1 How many millimetres are there in 2.5 cm?

2 Change these lengths into centimetres.

   (a) 2 m   (b) 1.6 m   (c) 70 mm   (d) 67 mm   (e) 3.61 m

3 Change these lengths into metres.

   (a) 400 cm   (b) 780 cm   (c) 3 km   (d) 7.82 km   (e) 0.6 km

4 Change 7300 m into kilometres.

5 Put each set of lengths in order, shortest first.

   (a) 50 m   800 cm   4 km   (b) 4 m   5 cm   120 mm

   (c) 0.2 m   3.5 cm   28 mm   (d) 7400 cm   900 m   0.5 km

6 Whooper swans sometimes fly at a height of 8230 m.
  How high is this in kilometres?

7 A common flea is 1.5 mm long.

   (a) In millimetres, how long is a line of 100 fleas?

   (b) Give your answer in centimetres.

8 Jane has a ribbon that is 3 metres long.
  She cuts off a piece that is 56 cm long.
  What length of ribbon is left?

9 A bee hummingbird weighs 1.6 g.
  How much would 1000 bee hummingbirds weigh in kilograms?

10 Which is heavier, 0.7 kg or 800 g?

11 (a) Change 1890 g to kilograms.   (b) Change 0.61 kg to grams.

12 (a) Change 1.94 litres to millilitres.   (b) Change 9760 ml to litres.

13 Janet buys 8 cartons of orange juice, each holding 200 ml.
  How many litres of orange juice does she buy altogether?

14 Pritti has two bags of potatoes.
  One weighs 2.5 kg and one weighs 850 g.
  In kilograms, what weight of potatoes does she have in total?

15 Sue has a bottle that holds 0.25 litres of olive oil.
  A teaspoon is 5 ml.
  How many teaspoons of oil are in the bottle?

17 Working with expressions 1

A Simplifying expressions such as $4 + 2n - 3 + n$

1 Simplify each of these expressions.

(a) $n + n + n + n + n$ (b) $x + x + x$ (c) $2e + 4 + e$

(d) $5 + 2j + 6$ (e) $m + 2 + 2m + 3$ (f) $7g + 3 + 5 + 3g$

(g) $20h + 4 + 10h + 7$ (h) $4 + 5k + 1 + k$ (i) $w + 2 + 2w + 5w + 8$

2 Write an expression for the perimeter of each shape.
Write each expression as simply as possible.

(a)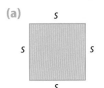

(b)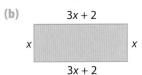

(c)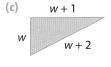

(d)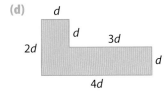

3 Work out an expression for each length marked **?**.

(a)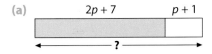

(b)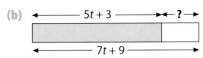

4 Simplify each of these expressions.

(a) $2x + x + 5 - 2$ (b) $3n + 7 + 7n - 1$ (c) $9 + 2v + 8v - 5$

(d) $2k + 5k - 2 + 7$ (e) $4b - 2 + 3b + 8$ (f) $2w + 3w + 5 - 8$

(g) $7q + q - 5 - 2$ (h) $h + 6h - 7 + 1$ (i) $3m - 9 + 6m + 4$

*5 Look at the grid of expressions.

(a) (i) Add up the expressions in row A
and simplify the result.

(ii) Repeat (i) for rows B and C.

(b) (i) Add up the expressions in column P
and simplify the result.

(ii) Repeat (i) for columns Q and R.

(c) What do you notice?

(d) (i) Make a grid of numbers by replacing each expression
with its value when $x = 10$.

(ii) Find the total of each row and column in this grid.

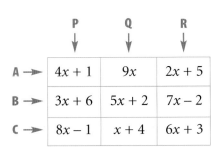

1 What is the value of each expression when $n = 3$?

   (a) $7 - n$ (b) $14 - n$ (c) $9 - n$ (d) $4 - n$

2 Find the value of each expression when $x = 4$.

   (a) $11 - 2x$ (b) $14 - 3x$ (c) $25 - 4x$ (d) $8 - 2x$

3 Given that $k = 7$, find the value of

   (a) $10 - k$ (b) $k - 10$ (c) $15 - k$ (d) $k - 15$

1 Simplify each of these.

   (a) $5a - 2a$ (b) $7n - n$ (c) $4x + 3x - 2x$

   (d) $7p - 3p + p$ (e) $8d - 4d - 2d$ (f) $5y - y - 3y$

2 Simplify each of these.

   (a) $10 + 6x - 3x$ (b) $3n + 1 - n$ (c) $6y - 3 - 2y$

   (d) $8 - 3m + 5m$ (e) $6 - 3k + 9k$ (f) $5a - 8 - 4a$

3 Find four pairs of equivalent expressions.

Ⓐ $3 + n - 5n$ Ⓑ $3 - 3n + n$ Ⓒ $3 - 4n$ Ⓓ $n + 3 - 6n$

Ⓔ $3 - 5n$ Ⓕ $3 - 7n - 2n$ Ⓖ $3 - 9n$ Ⓗ $3 - 2n$

4 Simplify each of these.

   (a) $1 + 3n - 5n$ (b) $3 - x + 5x$ (c) $4 - 3h - 5h$

   (d) $1 - k - k$ (e) $4p - 2p + 3 + 2$ (f) $3a + 7 - a - 2$

   (g) $4 + 3b + 1 - 2b$ (h) $10 + 2d - 1 - 4d$ (i) $8 - 2m - 3 - m$

5 Write down and simplify an expression for the perimeter of each shape.

(a)
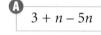
$7x - 5$

$3x$ $3x$

$7x - 5$

(b)
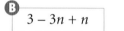
$4 - k$

$k + 3$

$4k$

$8 - 3k$

(c)
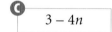
$10 - 3s$

$8 - 2s$

s

Mixed practice 2

You need centimetre squared paper.

1 This table shows the ages of people using a swimming pool
  on a Sunday morning.

Ages	Frequency
0–19	15
20–39	10
40–59	6
60–79	1

  (a) How many people aged 40 or over used the pool?

  (b) How many people altogether used the pool?

  (c) What is the modal age group?

  (d) Draw a bar chart to show the information.

2 Work out each of these. Show any working clearly.

  (a) 486 + 189   (b) 486 − 189   (c) 57 × 8   (d) 330 ÷ 5

  (e) 1.7 + 6.54   (f) 6.7 − 1.25   (g) 3.75 × 4   (h) 6.15 ÷ 5

3 Barry makes necklaces.
  Here are three different sizes.

Size 1   Size 2

Size 3

  (a) How many beads would be needed
      to make a size 4 necklace?

  (b) Copy and complete this table.

Size of necklace	1	2	3	4	5	10
Number of beads	6	11				

  (c) Which of these expressions is correct for
      the number of beads in a size n necklace?

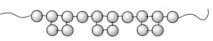

  $3n + 3$ $6n$ $5n + 1$

  $2n + 4$ $4n + 2$

  (d) What size necklace will use 41 beads?
      Show all your working.

4 Write each of these lists of temperatures in order, lowest first.

  (a) 2°C, ⁻3°C, 1°C, ⁻6°C, 5°C   (b) 2.5°C, ⁻1.5°C, 0°C, 3.5°C, ⁻3.5°C

5 Jane has 1.4 litres of water in a bottle.
  She pours 600 ml of this water into a jug.
  How much water is left in the bottle?

6 This solid is made from 8 centimetre cubes.

  (a) Is it a prism?

  (b) How many planes of symmetry does the solid have?

  (c) Draw a full-size plan view, front view and
      side view of the solid.

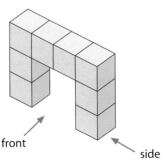

front

side

7 Write these in order, smallest first. $\frac{1}{3}$, 65%, 0.25, 20%, $\frac{3}{4}$

8 On centimetre squared paper draw a grid with both axes numbered from 0 to 7.
Then draw the parallelograms with these coordinates and find their areas.

(a) (0, 0) (3, 0) (4, 2) (1, 2)   (b) (5, 1) (7, 3) (7, 7) (5, 5)

9 Work these out.

(a) $7 + {}^-4$ (b) ${}^-6 + {}^-4$ (c) $1 - 9$ (d) $1 - {}^-2$ (e) $3 \times {}^-2$

10 Write down and simplify an expression for the perimeter of each of these.

(a)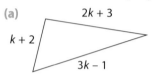

(b)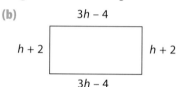

(c)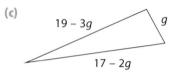

11 Copy and complete this table with
the correct equivalents.

Fraction	Decimal	Percentage
$\frac{1}{4}$		
	0.1	
		3%

12 Choose from the box the unit that would be
most appropriate to use when measuring

(a)   the weight of a person

(b)   the volume of a tropical fish tank

(c)   the weight of a teaspoon of flour

(d)   the volume of a teaspoon of water

grams
kilograms
tonnes
millilitres
litres
cubic metres

13 The average rainfall over the UK in June 2007 was 134.5 mm.
How many centimetres of rain is this?

14 Find the value of each expression when $n = 5$.

(a) $4n - 7$ (b) $2(n + 1)$ (c) $8 - n$ (d) $15 - 2n$

15 Ann and Beth are high-jumpers.
They keep a record of their last few jumps, in metres.

Ann	1.56	1.49	1.65	1.48	1.57
Beth	1.87	1.34	1.81	1.38	

(a)   Copy and complete the table on the right.

(b)   Which high-jumper would you pick for a competition?
Give two reasons for your choice.

	Mean	Range
Ann	1.55 m	0.17 m
Beth		

18 Graphs of changes over time

A Noise level

1 The graph shows the noise levels at the start of a pantomime.

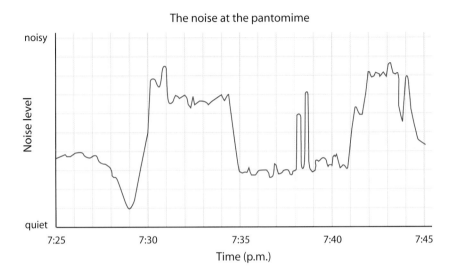

The noise at the pantomime

(a) The audience went very quiet as the lights were dimmed before the start.
When was this?

(b) The orchestra started the pantomime by playing some music just before
the story teller came on stage.

   (i)   For about how long were the orchestra playing at the start?

   (ii) At what time were the orchestra the loudest during this time?

(c) The story teller talked to the audience for about 3 minutes.
Then she got them to practise shouting at the wicked ogre.

   (i)   When did they first shout at the ogre?

   (ii) How many times did they shout at the ogre?

(d) The story teller talked a little longer and then she sang a song.
It was quite loud.
When did she start singing the song?

(e) At the end of the song the audience clapped loudly.

   (i)   When did the audience clap?

   (ii) About how long did the song last?

1 This graph shows the temperature inside Julie's car during 24 hours in summer.

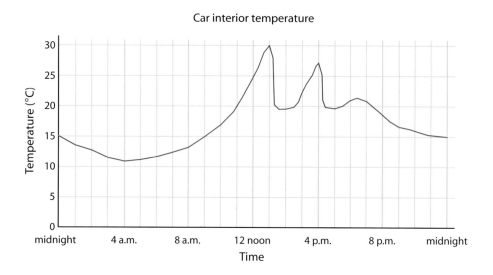

Car interior temperature

The car is fitted with air-conditioning.
When the air-conditioning is turned on, it lowers the temperature inside the car quite quickly.

(a) Estimate the temperature inside the car at

   (i) 8 a.m.   (ii) 4 p.m.   (iii) 10 p.m.

(b) At what time did the temperature first reach 25 °C?

(c) (i) What was the highest temperature in this 24 hours?

   (ii) At what time was this highest temperature reached?

(d) (i) Estimate the lowest temperature in this 24 hours.

   (ii) At what time was the temperature at its lowest point?

(e) For about how long was the temperature in the car above 15 °C?

(f) During that day Julie used the car to go shopping.
When she got in the car she turned on the air-conditioning.

   (i) When did she get in the car to go shopping?

   (ii) About how long do you think she spent at the shops?
   Explain your answer carefully.

   (iii) When did she get in the car to return home from the shops?

19 Chance

A Probability as a fraction

1 This fair spinner is spun once.

   (a) On which colour is it most likely to stop?

   (b) What is the probability it stops on

       (i) blue   (ii) white   (iii) yellow

   (c) What is the probability that it stops on a colour that is not white?

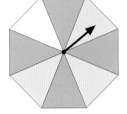

2 Seven balls numbered 1 to 7 are placed in a lottery machine.

   One ball is released.
   What is the probability that the number on it is

   (a) 5   (b) even   (c) not 6

   (d) 6 or 7   (e) smaller than 3   (f) 8

3 There are 6 blue cubes and 9 red cubes in a box.

   You take one of the cubes out of the box without looking.
   What is the probability that the cube is

   (a) blue   (b) red   (c) green

4 A bag contains 3 dark chocolate cookies, 5 raisin cookies and 4 white chocolate cookies.

   You take a cookie from the bag without looking.
   What is the probability that you pick

   (a) a dark chocolate cookie   (b) a raisin cookie

   (c) a chocolate cookie   (d) a cookie that is not a white chocolate one

5 These cards have pictures of black, grey and white shapes on one side.
   The cards are shuffled and placed picture side down.

   A card is turned over at random.
   What is the probability that the shape on the card is

   (a) black   (b) white

   (c) a square   (d) a triangle

   (e) not white   (f) not a circle

1 Two unbiased spinners with crown, star, diamond and pearl symbols are spun.

(a) Copy and complete this list of all the possible outcomes.

First spinner	Second spinner
Crown	Crown
Crown	Star

(b) How many outcomes are there altogether?

(c) For these spinners, what is the probability that

(i) both show a crown   (ii) both show a diamond

(iii) both show the same symbol   (iv) both show different symbols

2 The arrows on these two unbiased spinners are spun.

(a) Copy and complete this list of all the possible outcomes.

First spinner	Second spinner
1	2
1	

(b) How many outcomes are there altogether?

(c) What is the probability that the spinners show

(i) 1 and 2   (ii) two even numbers

(iii) two odd numbers   (iv) two different numbers

3 These four cards are shuffled and placed face down.

A card is chosen at random.
The card is returned to the pack and it is shuffled again.
A second card is chosen at random.

(a) Make a list of all the possible outcomes.

(b) How many outcomes are there altogether?

(c) What is the probability that

(i) both cards show the letter P

(ii) both cards show the same letter

(iii) one of the cards (but not both) shows a Q

(iv) one of the cards shows an R and one shows an S

c Using a grid

1 Two bags, A and B, each contain five numbered discs that are all the same size.

Bag A   Bag B

A disc is drawn at random from each bag.
The numbers are added together to get a score.

(a) Copy and complete the table to show all the possible scores.

(b) What is the probability that the score is

   (i)   8   (ii)   less than 6

   (iii)   an even number   (iv)   greater than 12

				Bag A		
	+	1	2	3	4	5
Bag B	1		3			
	3					
	5					
	7			10		
	9					

2 Matthew spins two five-sided spinners, each numbered 1, 2, 3, 4, 5.
He finds the **difference** between the numbers to get his score.

(a) Copy and complete the table to show all the possible scores.

(b) Which score is most likely?

(c) What is the probability of scoring 0?

(d) What is the probability that the score is greater than 2?

(e) What is the probability of scoring either 1 or 2?

				First spinner		
		1	2	3	4	5
Second spinner	1		1			
	2					
	3					
	4	3				
	5					0

3 One four-sided spinner is numbered 1, 2, 3, 4.
Another is numbered 3, 4, 5, 6.

Both spinners are spun and the numbers are **multiplied** together to get a score.

(a) Copy and complete this table.

(b) Which score is most likely?

(c) What is the probability that the score is

   (i)   4   (ii)   6

   (iii)   an odd number   (iv)   greater than 10

(d) What is the probability that the score is a square number?

			First spinner		
	×	1	2	3	4
Second spinner	3		6		
	4				
	5				
	6	6			

20 Area of a triangle and of composite shapes

You need centimetre squared paper in section A.

A Area of a triangle

1 Find the area of each shaded triangle on this grid of centimetre squares.
   Use the correct units in your answer.

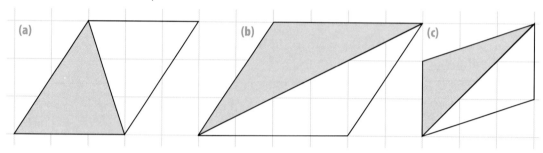

2 These triangles are drawn on centimetre squares. Find the area of each triangle.

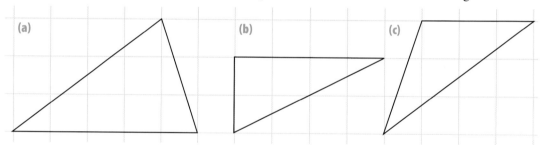

3 On centimetre squared paper draw three different triangles,
   each with an area of 8 cm².

4 Find the area of each of these triangles.

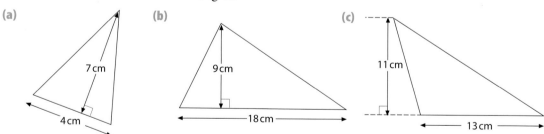

5 On centimetre squared paper draw three different triangles,
   each with an area of 17.5 cm².

1 These shapes are drawn on centimetre squared paper.
  Find the area of each shape, giving the correct units in your answer.
  Draw a sketch for each one to show how you did it.

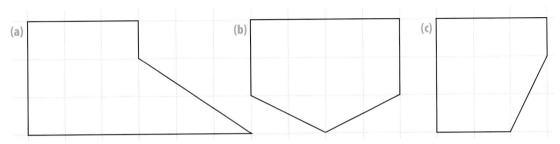

2 Find the area of each of these shaded shapes.
  Draw a sketch to show how you did each one.

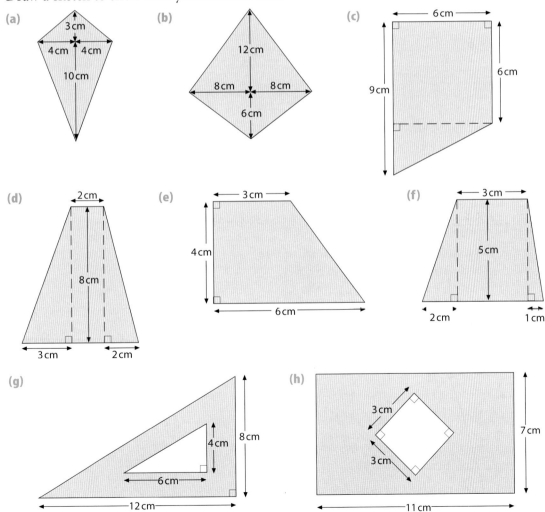

21 Working with percentages

A Review: fractions, decimals and percentages

1 Write these percentages as decimals.

(a) 15%　　　(b) 70%　　　(c) 24%　　　(d) 3%　　　(e) 9%

2 (a) Match each percentage with a fraction.

(b) What percentage is equivalent to the unmatched fraction?

$\frac{4}{5}$　$\frac{17}{20}$　$\frac{16}{25}$

$\frac{9}{20}$　$\frac{31}{50}$

45%　80%　62%　64%

3 Which is closer to 50%: 0.56 or $\frac{27}{50}$? Explain how you know.

4 Write each set of fractions, decimals and percentages in order, smallest first.

(a) 75%　0.6　$\frac{7}{10}$　66%　$\frac{2}{3}$　　　(b) $\frac{1}{10}$　0.15　1%　$\frac{1}{5}$　0.05

B Finding a percentage of an amount (mentally)

1 Work these out.

(a) 25% of £24　　(b) 50% of 32p　　(c) 75% of 12 litres　(d) 10% of 200 m

(e) 20% of £70　　(f) 30% of £40　　(g) 60% of 90 g　　(h) 80% of 110 kg

2 A fruit drink contains 40% apple juice.
How much apple juice is there in a 250 ml carton of the drink?

3 A standard box of cornflakes weighs 500 g.
A special-offer box has 25% extra free.
How much **extra** do you get in the special-offer box?

4 Work these out.

(a) 10% of £320　　(b) 5% of £320　　(c) 15% of £320　　(d) 35% of £320

5 Work these out.

(a) 5% of £120　　(b) 15% of 30 kg　　(c) 35% of 60 ml　　(d) 15% of £140

(e) 15% of 2000 m　(f) 45% of 400 g　　(g) 55% of £60　　(h) 95% of £40

6 Carlton's bus fare is 80p.
Fares are increased by 20%.

(a) How much extra does his fare cost?

(b) What is the new cost of his bus fare?

7 A packet of biscuits is described as '65% fat free'.

   (a) What percentage of the biscuits are fat?

   (b) If the packet weighs 500 g, how much fat do the biscuits contain?

8 In a sale, all prices are reduced by 25%.
Maddie buys a computer which originally cost £480.

   (a) What is 25% of £480?

   (b) How much does Maddie pay for the computer?

C Finding a percentage of an amount (with a calculator)

1 Calculate these.

   (a) 36% of 75   (b) 52% of £175   (c) 16% of £90   (d) 42% of 360 m

   (e) 26% of £65   (f) 18% of 89 kg   (g) 38% of £23   (h) 93% of 48 kg

2 A car bought for £12 600 had lost 53% of its value after three years.

   (a) Calculate 53% of £12 600.

   (b) What was the value of the car after three years?

3 A travel company advertises a discount of 12%.
What will be the discount on the following holidays?

   (a) A fly-drive holiday for £816   (b) An activity holiday for £482

4 This table shows the nutritional content of a breakfast cereal.

	Protein	Carbohydrate	Fat	Fibre
Percentage	11%	68%	12%	7%

How much of each nutrient is there in a 60 g serving of this breakfast cereal?

D Expressing one number as a percentage of another

1 Write these as percentages.

   (a) 12 out of 25   (b) 11 out of 20   (c) 70 out of 200   (d) 350 out of 1000

2 In a class of 25 students, 6 of them walk to school.
What percentage of the class walk to school?

3 In a bunch of 10 freesias, 2 are white, 3 are yellow and 5 are lilac.
What percentage of the bunch of freesias are

   (a) white   (b) yellow   (c) lilac   (d) not yellow

4 In a school of 400 pupils, 32 of them are left-handed.
What percentage are left-handed?

5 Henry asked students whether they had eaten breakfast that morning.
Out of 25 girls, 16 had eaten breakfast.
Out of 20 boys, 14 had eaten breakfast.

Had a larger percentage of girls or boys eaten breakfast? Explain how you decide.

E Expressing one number as a percentage of another (with a calculator)

1 Work these out as percentages.

(a) 54 out of 72   (b) 56 out of 350   (c) 168 out of 480   (d) 189 out of 450

2 I collected 75 apples from the tree in my garden. 36 of them were bad.

(a) What percentage were bad?   (b) What percentage were not bad?

3 Write these as percentages to the nearest 1%.

(a) 33 out of 45   (b) 56 out of 65   (c) 17 out of 24   (d) 320 out of 350

4 Nicola was given £45 for Christmas.
She wrote down how she spent the money.

CDs £19   Books £12   Stationery £6   Make-up £8

Work these out as percentages of the total amount. Check that they add up to 100%.

5 Khyle and Jack are practising archery.
Khyle misses the target on 5 out of 18 attempts.
Jack misses the target on 6 out of 24 attempts.

Who is more accurate? Explain how you know.

F Mixed questions

1 In a survey, a group of library users were asked why they had visited the library.

(a) How many people were asked in the survey in total?

(b) What percentage of this total visited to find information?

(c) What percentage visited to read a newspaper?

Reason	Number of people
Borrow/return books	34
Find information	16
Use the internet	12
Read a newspaper	7
Study	6

2 Judith works for 36 hours each week and earns £8.40 per hour.
She saves 15% of her earnings for a deposit on a flat.
How much money does she save each week?

22 Representing data

You need graph paper in sections C and EF.

A Two-way tables

B Two-way tables with grouped data

1 This table shows some results from a class survey.
Some of the numbers have been left out.

	Play a musical instrument	Do not play a musical instrument	Total
Boys	8	▦	14
Girls	▦	9	▦
Total	15	▦	30

(a) Copy and complete the table.

(b) How many boys are there in the class?

(c) What fraction of the girls play a musical instrument?

(d) What fraction of the class play a musical instrument?

2 These are the results of a survey on how often
students read newspapers.

	Male	Female
Every day	11	10
Sometimes	17	12
Never	28	22

(a) What is the total number of males in the survey?

(b) What percentage of the males sometimes read
a newspaper?

(c) What percentage of all the students never read a newspaper?

(d) What percentage of the students who never read a newspaper are female?

3 Ray did a survey on people with
appointments at a doctor's surgery.
He recorded their gender and
their age group.

	Age 0–17	Age 18–59	Age 60+	Total
Male	17	35	13	
Female	22	34	29	
Total				

(a) Copy the table and complete the totals.

(b) How many people aged 0–17 were there?

(c) How many people did Ray survey altogether?

(d) What fraction of the people were male?

(e) What percentage of the people were aged 60+?

(f) What fraction of the people were females aged 18–59?

C Pictograms and bar charts

1 Sue made this table of all the music CDs in her house.

Type of music	Rock	Metal	Classical	Jazz
Number of of CDs	30	25	50	12

Draw a pictogram for this data.

Use the symbol ⊙ to represent 10 CDs.

2 Aaron has carried out a survey on the number of bedrooms in houses in his area.
His results are shown in this bar chart.

(a) How many houses had two bedrooms?

(b) How many houses did Aaron use in his survey?

(c) What was the modal number of bedrooms in Aaron's survey?

(d) Aaron's cousin, Janice, does the same survey where she lives. Here are her results.

Bedrooms	1	2	3	4
Frequency	3	6	9	2

Draw a bar chart to show Janice's results.

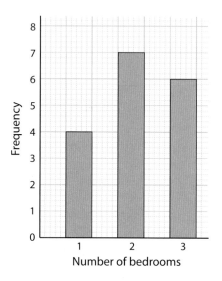

D Dual bar charts

1 This diagram shows the ten most popular uses of the internet for children in the UK in 2005.

(a) What was the most popular use for children aged 8–11?

(b) What was the least popular use for children aged 12–15?

(c) Make two comments comparing the use of the internet by the two age groups.

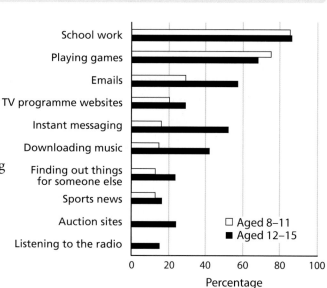

Source: Social trends

1 This time series graph shows the percentage of primary school classes with 31 or more pupils between 1989 and 2005.

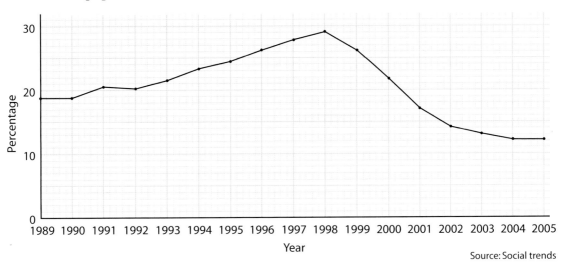

Source: Social trends

(a) What was the percentage of classes with 31 or more pupils in 1992?

(b) What was the percentage of classes with 31 or more pupils in 2000?

(c) In which year was the percentage of classes with 31 or more pupils greatest?

(d) Describe what the graph shows about the percentage of primary school classes with 31 or more children.

2 This table shows the annual Retail Price Index (RPI) from 1996 to 2006.

Year	1996	1997	1998	1999	2000	2001	2002	2003	2004	2005	2006
RPI	153	158	163	165	170	173	176	181	187	192	198

(a) Draw a line graph of the RPI between 1996 and 2006 using these scales.

(b) Between which two years was the rise in the RPI least?

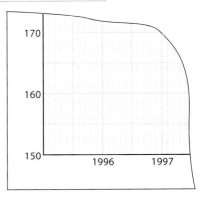

23 Ratio and proportion

A Recipes

Prawn pâté
(serves 4)

200 g peeled prawns
80 g butter
10 ml lemon juice
20 ml chopped parsley

Pink grapefruit sorbet
(serves 6)

250 g caster sugar
250 ml water
3 pink grapefruit
2 lemons

Mushroom risotto
(serves 2)

1 onion
100 g mushrooms
25 g butter
200 g risotto rice
1 litre vegetable stock
2 tablespoons Parmesan cheese

1 How much would you need of these ingredients to make the food described?

(a) Butter to make mushroom risotto for 4 people

(b) Caster sugar to make pink grapefruit sorbet for 18 people

(c) Mushrooms to make mushroom risotto for 8 people

(d) Chopped parsley to make prawn pâté for 2 people

2 (a) List the ingredients needed to make prawn pâté for one person.

(b) Use your answer to list the ingredients needed to make prawn pâté for

    (i) 6 people   (ii) 10 people   (iii) 15 people

3 (a) How much risotto rice do you need to make mushroom risotto for one person?

(b) Use your answer to work out how much risotto rice you would need
to make mushroom risotto for

    (i) 3 people   (ii) 5 people   (iii) 12 people

4 List the ingredients needed to make pink grapefruit sorbet for 9 people.

B Comparing prices

1 Here are some prices for cartons of orange juice.

(a) How much would 6 cartons bought separately cost?

(b) Does the multipack give you more for your money?

1-litre carton
70p

Multipack
6 cartons for £3.60

2 A 50 g bar of chocolate costs 39p.
A 250 g bar of chocolate costs £1.99.

(a) How many small bars would you need to get the same weight as a large bar?

(b) Do you save money by buying the large bar?

3 A 500 ml packet of washing liquid costs £1.49.
A 1500 ml bottle of washing liquid costs £4.49.

Which is better value for money, the packet or the bottle?

4 A 500 g box of cat biscuits costs £1.86.
A 2 kg bag of cat biscuits costs £7.35.

(a) How many boxes would you need to make the same weight as a bag?

(b) How much would these boxes cost?

(c) Do you save money by buying the bag?

c Unitary method

1 On a school trip, 80 children filled 2 coaches.

(a) How many children filled 1 coach?

(b) How many children would fill 5 coaches?

2 A tap fills an 8-litre bucket in 40 seconds.

(a) At the same rate how long will it take to fill a 1-litre container?

(b) How long will it take to fill a 15-litre bucket?

3 Megan cycles 45 km in 3 hours.
If she cycles at the same pace, how far can she cycle in 4 hours?

4 Frank drove 160 km travelling to work over a 4-week period.
At the same rate, how many kilometres would he drive travelling to work over a 9-week period?

5 This is a recipe for blue cheese dip for 3 people.
Write a recipe for blue cheese dip for 10 people.

Blue cheese dip (for 3)
60 ml soured cream
75 g blue Stilton cheese

6 Amy prepares packed lunches for groups going on day trips.
This is a list of food for packed lunches for 4 people.

Write a list of food for packed lunches for 7 people.

12 sandwiches
4 packets of crisps
4 pieces of fruit
2 litres of water

D Unit cost

1 A shop sells batteries for portable radios in packs of 4, 8, 12 and 20.

£3.00 4 PACK — £5.20 8 PACK — £7.20 12 PACK — £11.00 20 PACK

(a) For each pack, work out the cost of a single battery.

(b) Which pack is the best value for money?

(c) Which pack is the worst value for money?

2 In the following, use unit costs to work out which is cheaper.

(a) 5 kg for £1.35 or 4 kg for £1.12   (b) 8 litres for £4 or 10 litres for £5.50

(c) 9 kg for £27 or 2 kg for £5.80   (d) 7 metres for £8.75 or 8 metres for £9.60

3 Find the unit cost of these to the nearest penny.

(a) 3 metres of wood costing £7.99   (b) 6 kg of peanuts costing £3.99

(c) 25 kg of sand costing £2.99   (d) Orange juice costing £1.99 for 1.5 litres

4 Forever aftershave is sold in different sizes.

Large: 125 ml for £23.80   Standard: 75 ml for £14.30

Which size gives better value for money?
Show how you decide.

E Mixtures and ratio

1 Say whether each of these pictures shows a ratio of stars to circles of 3 : 1.
For those that do not, give the true ratio.

(a)   (b)   (c)   (d)

(e)   (f)   (g)

2 The ratio of apples to cherries in a pie mix is $1:5$.

   (a) How many cherries would you need to go with

      (i) 3 apples   (ii) 5 apples   (iii) 20 apples

   (b) How many apples would you need to go with

      (i) 10 cherries   (ii) 20 cherries   (iii) 50 cherries

3 First class and standard class seats on a train are in the ratio $1:10$.

   (a) How many standard class seats are there if the train has

      (i) 40 first class seats   (ii) 65 first class seats

   (b) How many first class seats are there if the train has

      (i) 300 standard class seats   (ii) 580 standard class seats

4 To make salad dressing, Tony uses 4 parts of oil for every part of vinegar.
   How much oil should he use with 30 ml of vinegar?

5 To make a pineapple and lime fruit drink, Amy uses pineapple juice
   and lime cordial in the ratio $4:1$.

   (a) If she uses 600 ml of pineapple juice, how much lime cordial will she need?

   (b) If she uses 250 ml of lime cordial, how much pineapple juice will she need?

   (c) How much pineapple juice would she need if she used a glassful of lime cordial?

6 To make orange and lemon drink you need oranges and lemons in the ratio $5:2$.

   (a) What is the ratio of lemons to oranges?

   (b) How many oranges would you need if you used 8 lemons?

   (c) How many lemons would you need if you used 25 oranges?

F Writing a ratio in its simplest form

1 Write these ratios in their simplest form.

   (a) $6:2$ (b) $12:30$ (c) $15:35$ (d) $200:250$

2 Write these as ratios in their simplest form.

   (a) A box contains 12 chocolate biscuits and 36 plain biscuits.

   (b) A swimming club has 40 female members and 60 males.

   (c) A company employs 350 full-time workers and 200 part-time workers.

3 Craig makes tropical juice by mixing 750 ml of orange juice with 250 ml of
   pineapple juice.

   (a) Write the ratio of orange juice to pineapple juice in its simplest form.

   (b) How much orange juice should he mix with 1 litre of pineapple juice?

24 Cuboids

A **Volume of a cuboid**
B **Cubic metres**

1 Find the volume of each of these cuboids.

(a)

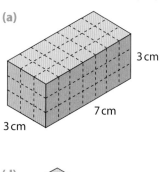

3 cm
7 cm
3 cm

(b)

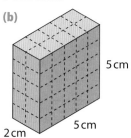

5 cm
2 cm
5 cm

(c)

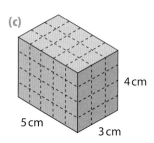

4 cm
5 cm
3 cm

(d)

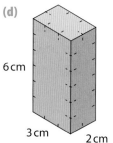

6 cm
3 cm
2 cm

(e)

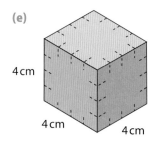

4 cm
4 cm
4 cm

(f)

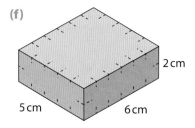

2 cm
5 cm
6 cm

(g)

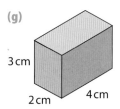

3 cm
2 cm
4 cm

(h)

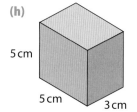

5 cm
5 cm
3 cm

(i)

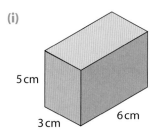

5 cm
3 cm
6 cm

2 A printer cartridge carton measures 10 cm by 5 cm by 6 cm.
What is the volume of the carton?

3 Find the volume of each of these packets.

(a)

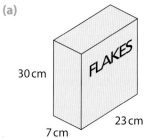

30 cm
7 cm
23 cm

FLAKES

(b)

19.6 cm
13 cm
4.2 cm

COFFEE FILTERS

(c)

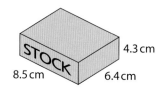

4.3 cm
8.5 cm
6.4 cm

STOCK

4 Each of these cuboids has a volume of 60 cm³.
Find the measurements labelled with letters.

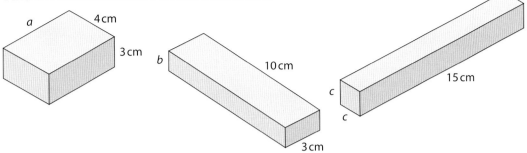

5 Find the volume of each of these cuboids in m³.

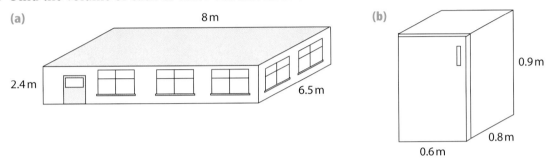

6 A store room measures 3 m long, 4 m wide and 2.5 m high.
Calculate the volume of the store room.

7 A block of icing has a volume of 48 cm³.
It is rolled out into a rectangle 10 cm by 24 cm.
How thick is the icing?

C Surface area

1 Below are sketches of a cuboid and its net.

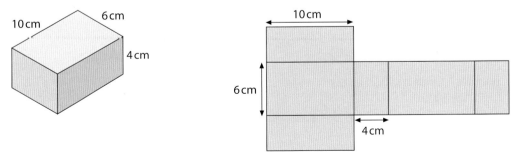

Calculate the surface area of this cuboid.

2 Find the surface area of each of these cuboids.

(a)

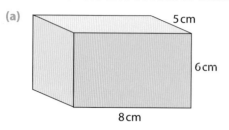

5 cm

6 cm

8 cm

(b)

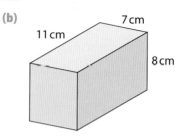

7 cm

11 cm

8 cm

(c)

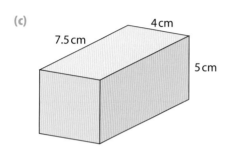

4 cm

7.5 cm

5 cm

(d)

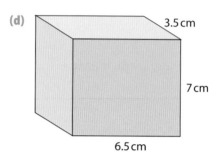

3.5 cm

7 cm

6.5 cm

D Volume of a solid made from cuboids

1 Find the volume of each solid.

(a)

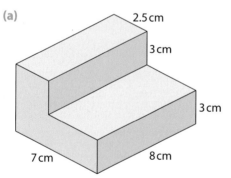

2.5 cm

3 cm

3 cm

7 cm

8 cm

(b)

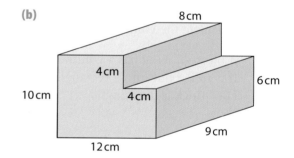

8 cm

4 cm

6 cm

10 cm

4 cm

12 cm

9 cm

(c)

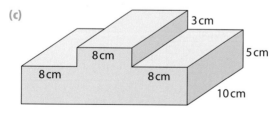

3 cm

8 cm

5 cm

8 cm

8 cm

10 cm

(d)

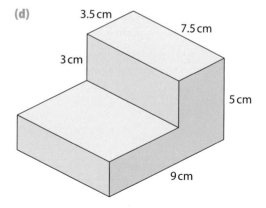

3.5 cm

7.5 cm

3 cm

5 cm

9 cm

Mixed practice 3

1   A box contains 5 mints and 10 fruit flavoured sweets.

   (a)   How many sweets are there in the box?

   (b)   I pick a sweet at random.
       What is the probability it is a mint?

2   This graph shows the midday temperature in Paris and Moscow for the first week of January.

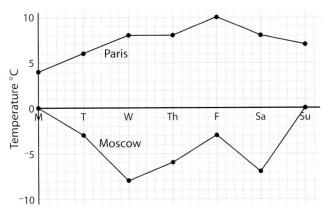

   (a)   What was the temperature at midday in Moscow on Friday?

   (b)   On what day was the difference in temperature between the two cities greatest?

   (c)   Find the mean and range of the midday temperatures in Paris for this week.

3   Find the shaded area in each of these shapes.

   (a)

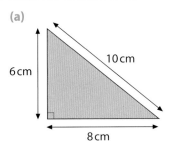

6 cm   10 cm   8 cm

   (b)

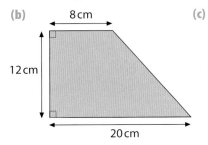

8 cm   12 cm   20 cm

   (c)

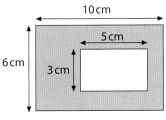

10 cm   5 cm   6 cm   3 cm

4   Jo has an unbiased six-sided dice and square spinner.
   She rolls the dice and spins the spinner.
   She adds the two numbers together to get a score.

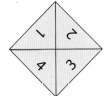

   (a)   Copy and complete this table to show all the possible scores.

   (b)   What is the probability that the score is 5?

   (c)   What is the probability that the score is more than 7?

Dice

+	1	2	3	4	5	6
1						
2						
3						
4	6					

Spinner

5 Write these ratios in their simplest form.

  (a) 8 : 4   (b) 6 : 9   (c) 36 : 8   (d) 10 : 25

6 'Value' orange squash comes in three sizes.
  Which size bottle works out cheapest?
  Explain your answer.

  500 ml   1.2 litre   3 litre
   72p   £1.50   £4.20

7 Write these as percentages.

  (a) 16 out of 100   (b) 35 out of 50   (c) 12 out of 25   (d) 68 out of 200

8 Soda pink paint is made by mixing red and white paint in the ratio 2 : 1.
  A painter has 3 litres of white paint and wants to make soda pink paint.

  (a) How much red paint will she need?

  (b) How much soda pink paint will she make?

9 Work out each of these. Give your answers to the nearest penny.

  (a) 17% of £24.50   (b) 38% of £49.70   (c) 7% of £12.60   (d) 15% of £37.77

10 This box of cereal is in the shape of a cuboid.

  (a) Calculate the volume of the box.

  (b) Calculate the surface area of the box.

  Include the correct units in your answers.

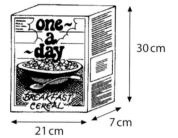

30 cm

21 cm   7 cm

11 Pete has a recipe for rhubarb jam where the ratio of rhubarb to sugar is 3 : 2.
   How much sugar would he use with 900 g of rhubarb?

12 A class survey of some students gave
   the results in the table.

	Boys	Girls
Left-handed	3	2
Right-handed	14	11

  (a) How many students are there in the class?

  (b) How many girls are there in the class?

  (c) What fraction of the class are left-handed?

  (d) To the nearest 1%, what percentage of the students in the class are boys?

  (e) To the nearest 1%, what percentage of the students in the class are right-handed?

  (f) What percentage of the right-handed students are girls?

25 Scatter diagrams and correlation

You need graph paper.

A Scatter diagrams
B Correlation

1 Two film critics watched some films.
They gave each film a score out of 10.

The scores are shown in the table.

| | Film | | | | | | | | | |
	A	B	C	D	E	F	G	H	I	J
Critic 1	6	8	2	4	4	9	7	6	7	10
Critic 2	6	7	2	6	5	10	4	8	7	8

(a) How many points did critic 1 give film F?

(b) Who gave 7 points to film B?

(c) Which film did critic 1 like the least?

(d) Which was critic 2's favourite film?

(e) Draw a scatter diagram on squared paper with both scales going from 0 to 10.

(f) Do you think that the film critics like similar films?
   Give a reason for your answer.

2 The table shows the measurements in centimetres of
the length and width of ten leaves taken from a tree.

| | Leaf | | | | | | | | | |
	A	B	C	D	E	F	G	H	I	J
Width (cm)	1.3	2.9	2.7	1.9	3.1	2.3	2.7	3.3	2.5	1.8
Length (cm)	3.2	6.6	4.8	4.0	6.5	4.9	5.5	7.0	5.0	3.0

(a) What is the length of leaf D?

(b) Which leaves have a width less than 2.0 cm?

(c) What is the length of the longest leaf?

(d) Is the longest leaf also the widest leaf?

(e) Plot the measurements on a scatter diagram
   with axes marked like this.

(f) What does the scatter diagram tell you about
   the connection between the lengths and
   the widths of these leaves?

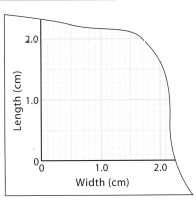

3 A group of students took a mathematics examination in year 6 and another mathematics examination in year 7.

Their results are shown in the table.

	Student											
	Ann	Boz	Carol	Dan	Ethan	Fiona	Gary	Hasha	Ian	Jade	Kabay	Liam
Year 6 mark (%)	93	84	62	76	55	98	66	51	88	61	58	79
Year 7 mark (%)	90	81	75	50	50	98	69	43	75	50	63	78

(a) What was Carol's mark in year 7?

(b) Who scored the same percentage mark in both years?

(c) Draw a scatter diagram on graph paper using these scales.

(d) Does this show positive, negative or zero correlation?

(e) Write a sentence describing the connection between the students' results in year 6 and year 7.

(f) Which student performed much better in year 6 than in year 7?

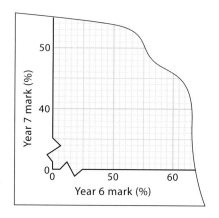

4 The table gives information taken from advertisements about the age of eight cars and their sale price.
All the cars are the same model.

Age (years)	3	9	7	6	13	10	5	2
Value (£)	6000	1000	2000	2500	500	2000	3500	6000

(a) Draw a scatter diagram on graph paper using these scales.

(b) What type of correlation does the graph show?

(c) Describe the relationship between the age and the value of the cars.

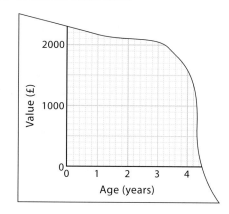

C Line of best fit

1 A magazine tested eight makes of walking shoes, which cost various amounts.
They gave each make a score based on comfort, water resistance and durability.

Cost (£)	30	60	65	50	70	80	70	50
Score	15	26	33	26	40	47	35	29

(a) Show the information on a scatter diagram
using these scales.

(b) Describe the correlation between the cost
and the score.

(c) Draw the line of best fit.

(d) A pair of walking shoes cost £40.
Use your graph to estimate a score.

(e) Another pair of walking shoes scored 42.
How much would you expect them to cost?

(f) A pair of walking shoes cost £15.
Use your graph to estimate a score.
How reliable do you think this estimate is?

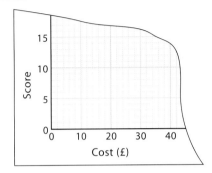

2 A football fan wanted to investigate any connection between
the number of points obtained by a football team and
the number of goals that were scored against them.

He looked at 12 teams in the league.

Points	69	65	52	44	38	55	50	44	53	36	33	24
Goals against	25	22	34	32	32	31	28	40	23	39	46	46

(a) Use the data to draw a scatter diagram on
graph paper using these scales.

(b) Draw a line of best fit.

(c) What does the graph tell you about the connection
between the points and goals against?

(d) Another team obtained 48 points.
Estimate how many goals were scored against them.

(e) If a team had 35 goals scored against them,
estimate how many points they obtained.

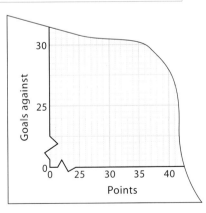

26 Square and cube numbers

A Squares and square roots

1 Which of the following are square numbers?

   4, 6, 9, 18, 25, 81, 90, 100

2 Find the value of each of these.

   (a) The square of 8   (b) 11 squared   (c) The square root of 100

3 Work these out.

   (a) 5^2 (b) 4^2 (c) $\sqrt{16}$ (d) $\sqrt{49}$ (e) $\sqrt{1}$

4 Use your calculator to work these out.

   (a) 19 squared   (b) 28^2 (c) The square root of 441

B Cubes and cube roots

1 List all the cube numbers that are less than 50.

2 What is the value of   (a) 5 cubed   (b) the cube root of 1000

3 Work these out.   (a) 7^3 (b) 11^3 (c) 8^3

4 Find the missing numbers.

   (a) ▦^{3} = 8   (b) ▦^{3} = 27   (c) ▦^{3} = 216   (d) ▦^{3} = 64

C Squares, cubes and higher powers

1 Work these out.

   (a) $3^2 - 1^3$ (b) $5^3 - 10^2$ (c) 2^4

2 Find all the numbers from 200 to 400 that are

   (a) square numbers   (b) cube numbers

3 Use the clues to find the numbers.

   (a)
   | A two-digit square number |
   | An odd number |
   | A multiple of 9 |

   (b)
   | A cube number |
   | A multiple of 4 |
   | Less than 10 |

   (c)
   | A three-digit square number |
   | Less than 200 |
   | The middle digit is 6 |

27 Surveys

B Designing a questionnaire

Some students are designing a questionnaire about mobile phone use.

1 Here are two versions of the first question. Which is better, and why?

A

| Which mobile phone network are you on? _____ |

B

| Tick the mobile phone network you are on. |
| O_2 ☐   Orange ☐   T-mobile ☐   Virgin ☐   Other ☐ |

2 Here are two versions of the second question. Which is better, and why?

A

| How much do you spend a month on mobile phone calls? _____ |

B

| How much do you spend a month on mobile phone calls? Tick the box |
| less than £10 ☐   £10–20 ☐   £20–30 ☐   More than £30 ☐ |

D Summarising results

The questionnaire about mobile phones was given to 20 boys and 20 girls. The results are shown here.

1 Copy and complete these two-way tables.

(a) Network

	O_2	Orange	T-mobile	Virgin	Other
Boys	5				
Girls	4				

(b) Monthly cost

	< £10	£10–20	£20–30	£30+
Boys	4			
Girls				

2 Draw a dual bar chart for each table. (Part of the chart for networks is shown here.)

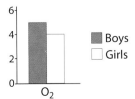

Boys

Network	Monthly cost
Virgin	£20–30
T-mobile	£20–30
T-mobile	£10–20
Orange	£30+
O_2	£20–30
Virgin	< £10
T-mobile	£30+
Virgin	£20–30
O_2	£20–30
Orange	£30+
O_2	£30+
Orange	£10–20
O_2	< £10
T-mobile	£20–30
T-mobile	£20–30
Orange	< £10
T-mobile	£20–30
Orange	£10–20
T-mobile	£30+
O_2	< £10

Girls

Network	Monthly cost
Virgin	£20–30
T-mobile	£20–30
Orange	£30+
T-mobile	£10–20
Virgin	< £10
O_2	£20–30
Virgin	< £10
Orange	£30+
Virgin	£20–30
O_2	£20–30
Orange	£30+
T-mobile	£30+
Orange	£30+
O_2	< £10
T-mobile	£10–20
Orange	£20–30
Orange	< £10
O_2	£20–30
Virgin	< £10
T-mobile	£30+

28 Imperial measures

1 Roughly how many feet are there in
   (a) 1 m   **(b)** 2 m   **(c)** 50 m   **(d)** 1 km

2 A garden measures 30 feet by 75 feet.
   What are these measurements in metres, approximately?

3 For each of these pairs, say which distance is longer.
   (a) 9 kilometres, 5 miles   **(b)** 30 kilometres, 20 miles
   (c) 100 km, 100 miles   **(d)** 16 km, 12 miles

4 Change these speed limits in miles per hour to kilometres per hour.
   (a)   **(b)**   **(c)**

   30   **50**   **70**

5 **(a)** Round these distances from Manchester to the nearest 10 miles.

   Birmingham   81 miles

   Derby   58 miles

   Leeds   39 miles

   Brighton   247 miles

   (b) Roughly what are these distances in kilometres?

6 Change these distances into miles.
   (a) 80 km   **(b)** 40 km   **(c)** 32 km   **(d)** 200 km

B **Weight**

1 What are these weights roughly in pounds (lb)?
   (a) 1 kg   **(b)** 3 kg   **(c)** 1.5 kg   **(d)** 4.5 kg

2 What are these weights roughly in kilograms?
   (a) 4 lb   **(b)** 20 lb   **(c)** 100 lb   **(d)** 1 lb

3 Which is the heavier in each of these pairs?
   (a) 5 lb, 5 kg   **(b)** 12 lb, 7 kg   **(c)** 80 lb, 30 kg   **(d)** $\frac{1}{2}$ lb, 300 g

4 Here is a recipe for marrow jam.
Write the recipe with the weights in kilograms.

Marrow	8 lb
Lemons	4
Sugar	6 lb

C Liquid measure

1 Roughly how many pints are there in
   (a) 1 litre   (b) 4 litres   (c) 18 litres   (d) $3\frac{1}{2}$ litres

2 Roughly how many litres are there in
   (a) 4 pints   (b) 18 pints   (c) 30 pints   (d) 9 pints

3 Approximately how many millilitres are there in
   (a) 2 pints   (b) 1 pint   (c) $\frac{1}{2}$ pint   (d) $\frac{1}{10}$ pint

4 One day a milkman delivered the following amounts of each type of milk.

   Gold top $4\frac{1}{2}$ gallons
   Silver top   18 gallons
   Semi-skimmed   16 gallons
   Skimmed   9 gallons

   (a) How many pints of each type of milk were delivered?

   (b) Approximately how many litres of each type of milk were delivered?

D Mixed questions

1 A book has a recipe to make 10 lb of apple jam.
   Roughly what weight of jam is this in kg?

2 Rewrite the following statements using the metric measurements
   indicated in the brackets.
   (a) I travelled 400 miles to get to Scotland. (kilometres)
   (b) The petrol tank in my car holds 15 gallons. (litres)
   (c) The weight of all the luggage we took on holiday was 100 lb. (kilograms)
   (d) My rubber plant has grown to a height of 9 feet. (metres)

3 Roughly how many miles are there in 320 km?

4 Roughly how many litres are there in 5 pints?

29 Navigation

You need an angle measurer for section D.

A Four-figure grid references and points of the compass

1 This is a map of some open countryside.

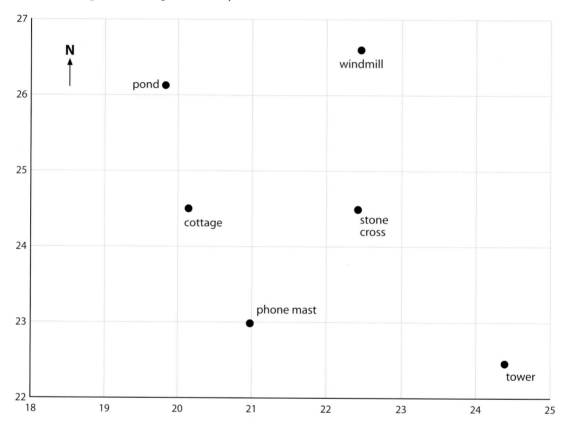

(a) Which landmark is in the square with grid reference 2422?

(b) Write down the four-figure grid reference for the square containing the pond.

(c) What landmark is north of the stone cross?

(d) What landmark is south-west of the stone cross?

(e) Christine walks in a straight line from the cottage to the windmill.
What compass direction is she walking in?

(f) Afzal walks directly from the cottage to the stone cross.
What compass direction is he walking in?

(g) A second cottage is to be built south-east of the windmill and north of the tower.
What is the grid reference of the square it will be in?

B Scales and points of the compass

1 This tourist map is drawn to a scale of 1 cm to 5 km.

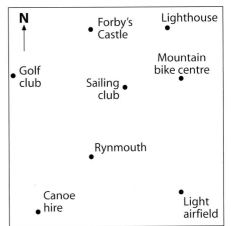

  (a) How far is it in real life, in a straight line, from

     (i) the light airfield to Forby's Castle

     (ii) Rynmouth to the lighthouse

     (iii) the mountain bike centre to the light airfield

  (b) What do you find 10 km north-east of
the sailing club?

  (c) How far is the golf club from Rynmouth?

  (d) In which compass direction is the golf club
from Rynmouth?

2

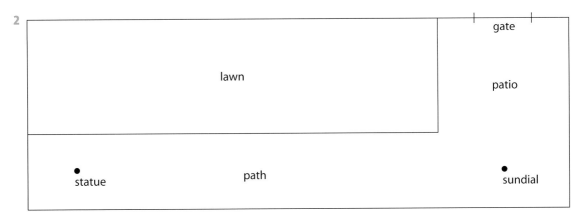

The garden plan above is drawn to a scale where 1 cm represents 2 m.

  (a) What would these measurements be in real life?

     (i) The width of the path   (ii) The distance from the gate to the sundial

     (iii) The length of the lawn   (iv) The distance from the statue to the sundial

  (b) The gardener makes a rectangular flower bed 8 m by 3 m in the lawn.
What size would it be on the plan?

  (c) A circular pond with diameter 4.6 m is dug into the lawn.
What would its diameter be on the plan?

3 A map is drawn using a scale of 1 cm to 25 km.
Change these distances on the map to actual distances in kilometres.

  (a) 7 cm   (b) 12 cm   (c) 25 cm   (d) 1.4 cm

4 A map is drawn using a scale of 1 cm to 50 km.
Change these actual distances to distances on the map in centimetres.

  (a) 200 km   (b) 850 km   (c) 1500 km   (d) 375 km

D Bearings

1

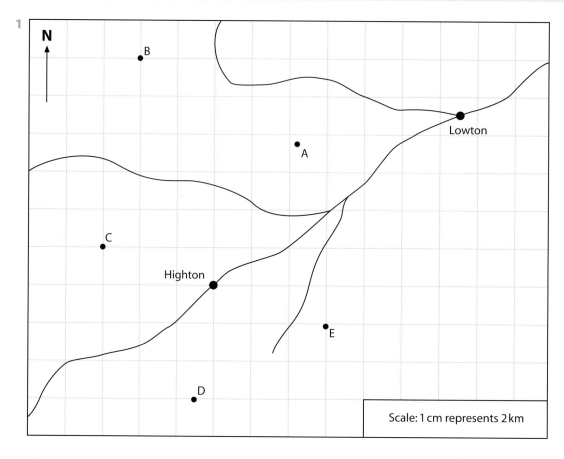

Scale: 1 cm represents 2 km

The map above shows five mountain peaks labelled A to E, and two towns, Highton and Lowton. It is drawn to a scale where 1 cm represents 2 km.

(a) How far is it in a straight line from Highton to Lowton in real life?

(b) Which mountain peak is on a bearing of 110° from Highton?

(c) What is the bearing of peak A from Highton?

(d) What is the bearing of peak D from Highton?

(e) A climber stands at the summit of peak B.

    (i) How far away is peak C?

    (ii) How far away is peak A?

    (iii) How much further away from the climber is peak C than peak A?

    (iv) What is the bearing of peak A from peak B?

    (v) What is the bearing of peak B from peak C?

(f) Which peak is on a bearing of 260° from Lowton?

(g) What is the bearing of peak D from peak E?

30 Rounding with significant figures

A Rounding a whole number to one significant figure
B Rounding a decimal to one significant figure

1 Round these numbers to one significant figure.

 (a) 621 (b) 78 (c) 4062 (d) 85 195 (e) 9456

2 Work out a rough estimate for each of these.

 (a) 48 × 19 (b) 72 × 31 (c) 184 × 22 (d) 58 × 285 (e) 108 × 386

3 A gardener needs to buy 32 fence panels at £21 each.

 (a) Estimate roughly the total cost of the fence panels.

 (b) Is your estimate bigger or smaller than the exact amount?
 How can you tell without working out the exact amount?

4 Round these numbers to one significant figure.

 (a) 56.2 (b) 0.512 (c) 0.0763 (d) 40.972 (e) 0.005 28

5 Rewrite each of these sentences, but round the number to one significant figure.

 (a) The world's longest cable suspension bridge has a main span of 1991 m.

 (b) The world's fastest train travelled at 574.8 kilometres per hour.

 (c) The world's smallest spider has a length of 0.43 mm.

 (d) The world's smallest fish has a length of 0.0079 m.

C Multiplying decimals

1 Copy these and fill in the missing numbers.

 (a)
```
3 × 4 = 12
3 × 0.4 = ...
0.3 × 0.4 = ...
```
 (b)
```
8 × 4 = 32
8 × 0.4 = ...
0.8 × 0.4 = ...
```
 (c)
```
4 × 5 = 20
4 × 0.5 = ...
0.4 × 0.5 = ...
```

2 Work these out.

 (a) 0.2 × 0.8 (b) 0.6 × 0.1 (c) 0.5 × 0.9 (d) 0.2 × 0.2

3 (a) Write down the answer to 2 × 12.

 (b) Now write down the answer to each of these.

 (i) 2 × 1.2 (ii) 2 × 0.12 (iii) 0.2 × 12 (iv) 0.2 × 0.12

4 You are told that $34 \times 45 = 1530$.
Write down the answer to each of these.

(a) 3.4×45 (b) 34×0.45 (c) 3.4×4.5 (d) 0.034×45 (e) 0.34×0.45

5 Work these out.

(a) 30×0.5 (b) 400×0.2 (c) 0.8×500 (d) 0.6×0.6 (e) 900×0.9

D Rough estimates with decimals

1 Work out a rough estimate for each of these.

(a) 3.12×0.625 (b) 0.723×19.5 (c) 4.89×0.032 (d) 318.5×0.378

2 52 people are going by coach to a theme park. They each pay £21.50.

(a) Estimate roughly the total amount paid.

(b) Is your rough estimate bigger or smaller than the exact amount?
How can you tell without working out the exact amount?

3 Jake measures the length and width of a rectangular room.
He says the length is 6.82 metres and the width is 3.85 metres.

(a) Estimate roughly the area of the floor of the room.

(b) Is your rough estimate bigger or smaller than the actual area?

4 Work out a rough estimate for each of these.

(a) $\dfrac{38.8 \times 0.324}{2.96}$ (b) $\dfrac{53.6 \times 0.763}{3.84}$ (c) $\dfrac{213.3 \times 0.603}{27.88}$ (d) $\dfrac{0.0126 \times 768}{3.74}$

E Rounding answers

1 Use a calculator to work these out.

(a) 2.51×3.45, answer to 2 d.p.   (b) 0.456×23.78, answer to 1 d.p.

(c) 4.235×8.76, answer to 2 d.p.   (d) 0.0684×1.27, answer to 3 d.p.

2 Polly buys 10.5 metres of ribbon costing £0.93 per metre.

(a) Work out a rough estimate of the total cost.

(b) Use a calculator to find the total cost. Round it to the nearest penny.

3 Charlie weighs 8.5 stones. One stone is equivalent to 6.35 kg.
Work out Charlie's weight in kilograms. Give your answer to one decimal place.

4 Max buys 0.35 kg of salmon fillet costing £12.99 per kilogram.
Work out the total cost of the salmon, to the nearest penny.

31 Solving equations

B Seeing a balance puzzle as an equation

1 Here is a set of equations.

(a) $4x + 3 = 19$ (b) $3x + 4 = 19$ (c) $3x + 2 = 4x$ (d) $3x + 2 = x + 4$

For each equation

- give the letter for the balance puzzle below that matches it
- solve the puzzle and write down the solution in the form '$x = ...$'

C Solving an equation using balancing

1 Use balancing to solve these equations.
(Show your working clearly and check each answer.)

(a) $2x + 3 = 13$ (b) $5x + 6 = 21$ (c) $4x + 1 = 25$

(d) $7x = 2x + 20$ (e) $3x + 12 = 4x$ (f) $x + 14 = 8x$

2 (a) Write down an equation for this puzzle.
Use x to stand for the weight of a tin.

(b) Solve the equation to find
the weight of a tin.

3 Use balancing to solve these equations.

(a) $2x + 1 = x + 5$ (b) $4x + 3 = 3x + 6$ (c) $5x + 2 = x + 10$

(d) $4x + 3 = 2x + 13$ (e) $7x + 2 = 3x + 6$ (f) $5x + 1 = 2x + 10$

(g) $6x + 11 = 8x + 1$ (h) $3x + 13 = 6x + 4$ (i) $4x + 26 = 9x + 1$

E Undoing a subtraction in an equation

1 Solve these equations.

   (a) $x - 2 = 3$ (b) $x - 8 = 4$ (c) $2x - 2 = 4$

   (d) $3x - 2 = 10$ (e) $5x - 1 = 4$ (f) $4x - 1 = 19$

2 Solve these equations.

   (a) $2x - 1 = x + 4$ (b) $3x - 2 = x + 6$ (c) $2x + 4 = 5x - 2$

   (d) $x + 5 = 5x - 3$ (e) $4x - 6 = 2x + 8$ (f) $3x + 5 = 7x - 11$

*3 Solve these equations.

   (a) $2x = 6x - 8$ (b) $5x - 10 = 3x - 2$ (c) $6x - 16 = x - 1$

F Decimal, negative and fractional solutions

1 Solve these equations.

   (a) $4y = 6$ (b) $10p + 3 = 4$ (c) $5n - 3 = 1$

   (d) $b + 6 = 4$ (e) $y + 5 = 1$ (f) $2a + 5 = 1$

   (g) $3x + 2 = x + 5$ (h) $7d - 1 = 3d + 9$ (i) $k + 10 = 6k + 7$

   (j) $p + 6 = 3p + 8$ (k) $5s + 6 = 3s + 2$ (l) $3m + 2 = 2m - 1$

2 Solve these equations. Write each answer as a fraction.

   (a) $4x + 5 = 6$ (b) $5x + 3 = 2x + 4$ (c) $8x - 2 = x + 2$

G Problem solving

1 (a) Write an expression for the sum of
     the angles marked in this triangle.
     Give your answer in its simplest form.

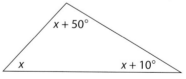

   (b) The angles of a triangle add up to 180°.
     Write down an equation in x and use it to find the value of x.

2 (a) Find an expression in terms of x for
     the perimeter of this pentagon.
     Give your answer in its simplest form.

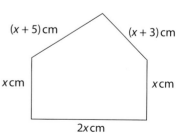

   (b) The perimeter of the pentagon is 62 cm.
     Write an equation and solve it to find the value of x.

   (c) Find the length of the longest side.

32 **Written calculation 2**

A Multiplying by a two-digit number

1 Work these out.

    (a) 14×18 (b) 23×41 (c) 42×35 (d) 56×79

2 Work these out.

    (a) 56×73 (b) 74×82 (c) 68×62 (d) 83×91

3 Work these out.

    (a) 175×21 (b) 432×29 (c) 704×92 (d) 231×83

4 Whyford Supporters Club took 18 coaches of fans to an away match.
Each coach carried 41 supporters.

    (a) Do an approximate calculation to estimate how many supporters travelled by coach.

    (b) Calculate the exact number of supporters who travelled by coach.

B Dividing by a two-digit number

1 Work these out.

    (a) $266 \div 14$ (b) $378 \div 18$ (c) $594 \div 22$ (d) $384 \div 24$

2 Work these out.

    (a) $713 \div 23$ (b) $912 \div 48$ (c) $901 \div 53$ (d) $999 \div 37$

3 Work these out.

    (a) $1152 \div 36$ (b) $2048 \div 64$ (c) $1998 \div 37$ (d) $1508 \div 58$

4 A seed merchant packs his tomato seeds into small and large packets.
He can put 18 seeds into each small packet and 32 seeds into each large packet.
He has 1440 seeds.

    (a) How many small packets could he make?

    (b) How many large packets could he make?

5 Margaret has 158 CDs.
She keeps them in racks that hold a maximum of 24 CDs.

    (a) How many racks can Margaret fill?

    (b) How many CDs are left over?

C Mixed questions

1 James uses pieces of string 15 cm long to tie up his rubbish bags.
   How many rubbish bags can he tie up with 840 cm of string?

2 A drama group is putting on a play.
   The theatre they use has 52 rows of 36 seats.
   Calculate the number of seats in the theatre.

3 A bottle of cola costs 89p.
   What is the total cost of 15 bottles of cola?

4 4 and 5 make a factor pair for 20 because $4 \times 5 = 20$.

   (a) 31 is one number in a factor pair for 1457.
        Find the other number in the factor pair.

   (b) 42 and 27 make a factor pair for a number.
        What is the number?

5 Jamie's car travels 11 miles on every litre of petrol.
   Last month he drove 396 miles.

   (a) How many litres of petrol did he use?

   (b) If a litre of petrol costs 92p, how much did Jamie spend on petrol last month?

6 A large bottle holds 2500 ml of orange squash.

   (a) How many drinks, each using 85 ml of squash, can be made from the bottle?

   (b) How much orange squash is left over?

7 A bathroom wall is 360 cm long and 270 cm high.
   It is covered in rows of square tiles each measuring 15 cm by 15 cm.

   (a) How many rows of tiles are there?

   (b) How many tiles are there in each row?

   (c) How many tiles are there on the wall?

   (d) Each tile costs 36p.
        What is the total cost of the tiles?

360 cm

270 cm

8 Marcia ran a stall at the school fair.
   She sold cakes for 35p each and drinks for 20p each.
   She sold 52 cakes and 145 drinks.
   How much money did she take altogether?

Mixed practice 4

You need graph paper.

1 These questions were included in a survey about pocket money.

A
> Children these days don't get enough pocket money.
>
> Do you agree?   Yes ☐   No ☐

B
> How much pocket money do you get?
>
> Very little ☐   Quite a lot ☐

(a) Say what you think is wrong with each question.

(b) Write a better question B to find out how much pocket money children get.

2 An ice cream seller records the maximum daily temperature and the number of ice creams he sells each day.

Maximum temperature (°C)	22	26	25	27	25	20	24	26	28	27
Number of ice creams sold	85	102	94	103	92	72	89	100	107	105

(a) Show this data on a scatter diagram with axes marked like this.

(b) Draw a line of best fit.

(c) Describe the type of correlation between the maximum temperature and the number of ice creams sold.

(d) The maximum temperature for the next day is 23 °C.
Estimate the number of ice creams that he sells on that day.

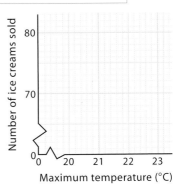

3 What is the area of a rectangular floor that measures 19 m by 31 m?

4 This is the plan of a room, drawn to a scale where 1 cm represents 2 m.

(a) How long is the wall AB in the real room?

(b) Find the area of this room in m².

(c) If the door is 1 m wide, find the total length of skirting board needed to go round the edge of this room.

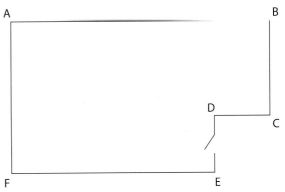

5 List all the square numbers that are less than 200.

6 Round the number in this headline to one significant figure.

7 A map is drawn to a scale of 1 cm to 50 km.
Change a real-life distance of 325 km to a length on this map.

8 Solve these equations.

(a) $n + 12 = 2n + 4$ (b) $8n + 3 = 2n + 15$ (c) $2n - 5 = 1$

(d) $3n - 1 = n + 5$ (e) $4n + 1 = 5n - 4$ (f) $5n + 11 = 3n + 7$

 9 Which is heavier, 5 lb or 3 kg?

10 Jay is planting broad bean seedlings in rows.
He plants 21 seedlings in each row.
He has 861 seedlings to plant.
How many rows can he plant?

11 Work out 0.4×0.1.

12 What is the value of 10 cubed?

13 (a) Work out 24×15.

(b) Hence write down the answer to 0.24×150.

14 This diagram shows a corner of a square made from 64 dots.
How many dots are along one edge?

15 Roughly how many litres are there in

(a) 2 pints   (b) 12 pints   (c) 2 gallons

16 (a) Write down and simplify an expression for
the perimeter of this pentagon in terms of x.

(b) The perimeter of the pentagon is 50 cm.
Write down an equation in x.
Use it to find the value of x.

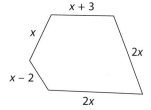

 17 Yasmin completes a 25 mile cycle ride.
About how many kilometres is this?

18 Work out a rough estimate for each of these.
Show your working clearly.

(a) 48.95×5.34 (b) $59.3 \div 1.973$ (c) $\dfrac{97 \times 0.49}{1.89}$ (d) $\dfrac{0.147 \times 3977}{3.785}$

19 Find the value of $8^3 + 6^2$.

20 Solve the equation $4x + 5 = x + 6$ and write your answer as a fraction.

33 Sequences

A Continuing a sequence

1 For each of these sequences, the first four terms and the rule are given.
 Write down the next three terms of each sequence.

(a) 1   5   9   13   ...   Add 4 to the previous term.

(b) $1\frac{1}{2}$ 3   6   12   ...   Double the previous term.

(c) 1   4   13   40   ...   Multiply the previous term by 3 and add 1.

2 Work out the next two terms in each of these sequences.
 Write down the rule for finding the next term in your sequence.

(a) 3   8   13   18   ...

(b) 40   37   34   31   ...

(c) 5   10   20   40   ...

(d) 12   7   2   ⁻3   ...

(e) 11   8   5   2   ...

(f) 5 $4\frac{1}{2}$ 4 $3\frac{1}{2}$ ...

3 In this number pattern, you add the previous two numbers to get the next number.

    4   5   9   14   ...

 Write down the next two numbers in this pattern.

*4 A sequence starts   1   3   7   ...

 Jo says the next two terms are   13   21
 Peter says the next two terms are   15   31
 Explain why both Jo and Peter could be right.

B Describing numbers in some sequences

1 Match each sequence below with its correct description.

A   2   4   8   16   32   ...

B   6   12   18   24   30   ...

C   1   4   9   16   25   ...

D   1   3   6   10   15   ...

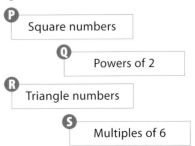

P   Square numbers

Q   Powers of 2

R   Triangle numbers

S   Multiples of 6

C Sequences from patterns

1 Here is a pattern made with matches.

  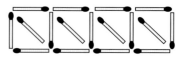

Pattern 1   Pattern 2   Pattern 3

(a) Copy and complete the table.

Pattern	1	2	3	4	5
Number of matches	9	13			

(b) Which pattern can be made with exactly 33 matches?

(c) Explain how you could work out the number of matches needed for pattern 10 without doing any drawing.

2 Here are some patterns of dots.

Pattern 1   Pattern 2   Pattern 3

(a) Draw pattern 4.

(b) Copy and complete the table.

Pattern	1	2	3	4	5
Number of dots	6	10			

(c) Write down the number of dots needed for pattern 10.
Explain how you found your answer.

3

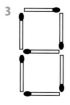 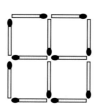 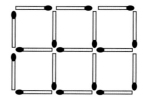

Shape 1   Shape 2   Shape 3

(a) Copy and complete this table for the shapes above.

Shape	1	2	3	4	5
Number of matches	7				

(b) How many matches would there be in shape 12?
Explain how you got your answer.

(c) Which shape is made from exactly 72 matches?

34 Problem solving with a calculator

A Which calculation?

1   The South West Coast Path is 630 miles long.
    Jeanette has walked 243 miles of the path.
    How many more miles has she to walk?

2   Each classroom in a school contains 32 chairs.
    If there are 27 classrooms, how many chairs are there altogether?

3   Six people have a picnic lunch.
    They agree to share the cost equally.
    They spend £14.80 on sandwiches, £8.46 on cakes and £4.28 on drinks.

    (a)   How much do they spend altogether?

    (b)   How much does each person pay?

4   Four adults and a child go to a theme park.
    The total cost of their tickets is £84.35.
    A child ticket costs £12.55.

    (a)   What is the total cost of the four adult tickets?

    (b)   How much does one adult ticket cost?

5   Jan buys some bottles of cola and a bottle of orange squash.
    The bottles of cola cost £1.19 each.
    The bottle of orange squash costs £1.49.
    The total cost is £9.82.

    (a)   What is the total cost of the bottles of cola?

    (b)   How many bottles of cola does Jan buy?

B Showing working

1   Gary buys a bed, two bedside tables and a wardrobe.
    The bed costs £345.50. The bedside tables cost £39.90 each.
    The total cost of all four things is £741.25.

    How much does the wardrobe cost?

2   Three people make cakes and sell them. They agree to share the profit equally.
    The ingredients for making the cakes cost £4.88.
    The cakes are sold for £12.35 altogether.

    How much profit does each person get?

3 The mileometer on Arnie's car read 45 928 miles at the start of the week.
During that week, Arnie used the car only to drive to and from work.
He drove to work and back four times.
At the end of the week the mileometer read 46 060 miles.

How far is it from Arnie's home to work?

4 Steve buys 4 coffees and 2 muffins for £9.40.
Maninder buys 3 coffees for £4.95.

What is the cost of a muffin?

5 A family of 2 adults and 2 children visit
the cinema at 6:30 p.m.

How much money do they save by buying
a family ticket rather than individual tickets?

Cinema prices		
	Before 5 p.m.	After 5 p.m.
Adult	£5.70	£6.60
Child	£4.20	£4.20
Family (2 adults, 2 children)	£16.80	£16.80

c Changing money to a different currency

Use these exchange rates in the questions below.

£1 = 15.60 Hong Kong dollars
£1 = 81.62 rupees (India)
£1 = 14.34 rand (South Africa)

1 Change £45.80 into rand.
Give the answer to the nearest rand.

2 Change 315 Hong Kong dollars to £, to the nearest penny.

3 (a) Marie goes to India. She changes £200 into rupees.
How many rupees does she get?

(b) When Marie leaves India she changes 1860 rupees into £.
How much does she get to the nearest penny?

4 In Hong Kong, Bharat sees a pocket TV on sale for 1270 dollars.
How much is this in £, to the nearest penny?

5 Ben has a mix of English and South African money.
He has £24.50 and 390 rand.

What is Ben's money worth

(a) in rand

(b) in pounds

35 Working with expressions 2

A Substituting into expressions such as $2a - b$

1 What is the value of each expression when $a = 4$ and $b = 3$?
  (a) $a + b$
  (b) $a - b$
  (c) $a + 5 - b$
  (d) $2a + b$
  (e) $3a - b$
  (f) $2b + a$
  (g) $2b - a$
  (h) $3b - 2a$

2 What is the value of each expression when $x = 2$ and $y = 7$?
  (a) $2x + y$
  (b) $2x + 3y$
  (c) $2y + 3x$
  (d) $4x - y$
  (e) $3y - x$
  (f) $5x - y + 4$
  (g) $y - 3x + 1$
  (h) $2x + 4y - 10$

B Simplifying expressions such as $3a + 2b + a + 5b$
C Simplifying expressions such as $3a + 2b + a - 5b$

1 Simplify each expression.
  (a) $2n + 3m + m + n$
  (b) $3r + s + 4r + 2s$
  (c) $5p + 2q + q + 3p$
  (d) $2a + 7 + 4b + a - 2$
  (e) $3g + 5 + 2f + 4 + 2g + f$
  (f) $7j - 3 + 2j + 4 + 3k + 2k$
  (g) $7x + 2 + 4x + 3y - 3$
  (h) $6p + 2q - 9 + p + 7$
  (i) $4h - 7 + 5g - 2 + h + g$

2 Simplify each expression.
  (a) $7a + 3b - 2a + b$
  (b) $8p + 7q + 2p - 6q$
  (c) $6c + 3d - 3c - d$
  (d) $3r - 2s + r + 4s$
  (e) $x - 4y + 3x + 7y$
  (f) $2m + 6n + 3m - 8n$
  (g) $2x - 5y + x + 3y$
  (h) $2w - 2v + 3w - 4v$
  (i) $10c - 2d - c - 3d$

3 Work out and simplify an expression for the perimeter of each of these.
  (a)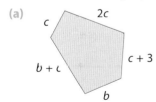
  (b)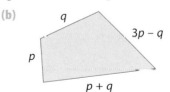
  (c)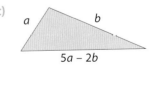

4 Simplify each expression.
  (a) $3m + 10 + n - 2m - 2n$
  (b) $6p - 2q + 4 - 4p + 3q - 2$

5 Find an expression for the length marked **?**.

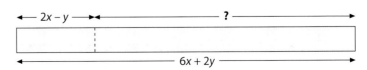

36 Calculating with negative numbers

A Adding and subtracting

1 Work these out.

(a) $5 - 9$ (b) $^-3 + 4$ (c) $^-6 - 1$ (d) $4 + ^-3$ (e) $^-10 + ^-3$

2 Find the missing number in each calculation.

(a) $8 + ? = 5$ (b) $7 + ? = ^-1$ (c) $? + ^-3 = ^-9$ (d) $? + ^-4 = 3$

3 In a magic square the numbers in each row, each column and each diagonal add to the same total.
Copy and complete these magic squares.

(a)

$^-3$		8
	2	
	7	

(b)

	3	$^-5$
	$^-2$	
1		

(c)

$^-4$	1	
3		
$^-2$		

4 Work these out.

(a) $6 - ^-2$ (b) $4 - ^-7$ (c) $^-5 - ^-8$ (d) $9 - ^-9$ (e) $0 - ^-7$

5 Choose pairs of numbers from the loop to make these calculations correct.

(a) $\blacksquare - \blacksquare = ^-4$ (b) $\blacksquare - \blacksquare = ^-5$

(c) $\blacksquare + \blacksquare = 1$ (d) $\blacksquare - \blacksquare = 1$

$\left(\; 1 \quad 5 \quad ^-3 \quad ^-4 \;\right)$

B Multiplying

1 Work these out.

(a) $5 \times ^-3$ (b) $^-4 \times 2$ (c) $^-6 \times 3$ (d) $^-2 \times ^-3$ (e) $6 \times ^-1$

(f) $^-2 \times ^-2$ (g) $^-8 \times ^-7$ (h) $^-4 \times ^-6$ (i) $3 \times ^-4 \times 2$ (j) $5 \times ^-2 \times ^-6$

2 Copy and complete these multiplication grids.

(a)

×	$^-1$	$^-3$	4
3	$^-3$		
$^-2$			
$^-5$			

(b)

×	$^-4$	6	8
2			
$^-3$			
$^-10$			

(c)

×		
2	$^-2$	
$^-3$	$^-6$	12
	$^-8$	

3 Find the missing number in each calculation.

(a) $8 \times ? = ^-24$ (b) $^-5 \times ? = 35$ (c) $? \times ^-6 = 36$ (d) $^-4 \times ? = 32$

C Dividing

1 Work these out.

   (a) $10 \div {}^-2$ (b) ${}^-20 \div 4$ (c) ${}^-18 \div {}^-9$ (d) ${}^-5 \times {}^-9$ (e) ${}^-4 \times 8$

   (f) ${}^-64 \div {}^-8$ (g) ${}^-50 \div 10$ (h) ${}^-5 \times {}^-10$ (i) $6 \div {}^-6$ (j) ${}^-9 \div {}^-9$

2 Find the missing number in each calculation.

   (a) ${}^-4 \times ? = 12$ (b) ${}^-70 \div ? = {}^-10$ (c) ${}^-8 \times ? = 40$ (d) ${}^-6 \times ? = 6$

   (e) $? \div {}^-7 = {}^-8$ (f) $90 \div ? = {}^-9$ (g) $? \times {}^-4 = 16$ (h) ${}^-48 \div ? = {}^-8$

3 Choose pairs of numbers from the loop to make these calculations correct.

   (a) ▓ $\div$ ▓ $= {}^-2$ (b) ▓ $\times$ ▓ $= {}^-12$ $\boxed{3 \quad {}^-4 \quad {}^-6 \quad {}^-24}$

   (c) ▓ $\div$ ▓ $= 4$ (d) ▓ $\times$ ▓ $= 24$

4 Use two numbers from $3, 5, {}^-5, {}^-20$ and either $\times$ or $\div$ to get the following results.

   (a) ${}^-15$ (b) 4 (c) 100 (d) ${}^-25$ (e) ${}^-1$

*5 Use two of these machines to make a number machine chain that gives

   (a) an output of 9 for an input of 6

   (b) an output of ${}^-4$ for an input of 4

   (c) an output of ${}^-8$ for an input of 12

D Negative square roots and cube roots

1 Work these out.

   (a) $({}^-2)^2$ (b) $({}^-6)^2$ (c) $({}^-4)^3$ (d) $({}^-9)^2$ (e) $({}^-8)^3$

2 Write down

   (a) (i) the positive square root of 64   (ii) the negative square root of 64

   (b) (i) the positive square root of 121   (ii) the negative square root of 121

3 Find two numbers to fit each statement.

   (a) ▓$^2 = 16$ (b) ▓$^2 = 9$ (c) ▓$^2 = 25$ (d) ▓$^2 = 100$

4 Find the cube root of each of these.

   (a) 64 (b) ${}^-64$ (c) 1000 (d) ${}^-125$ (e) 512

5 Copy and complete these.

   (a) $({}^-▓)^2 = 81$ (b) $({}^-8)^2 = $ ▓   (c) $(▓)^3 = {}^-64$ (d) $({}^-1)^▓ = {}^-1$

E Mixed questions

1 Work these out.

(a) $4 + {}^-9$ (b) $3 \times {}^-7$ (c) $3 - 10$ (d) $20 \div {}^-5$ (e) ${}^-3 \times {}^-6$

(f) $5 - {}^-1$ (g) ${}^-7 \times {}^-1$ (h) ${}^-2 - {}^-8$ (i) ${}^-24 \div 6$ (j) ${}^-30 \div {}^-5$

2 Work these out.

(a) $5 + {}^-2 + {}^-1$ (b) $5 - 4 - {}^-3$ (c) ${}^-5 \times 3 \times {}^-2$ (d) ${}^-1 \times {}^-2 \times {}^-3$

3 Calculate these.

(a) $(4 - 7) \times {}^-3$ (b) $2 \times ({}^-3 - 4)$ (c) $({}^-2 - {}^-3) \times 5$ (d) $(2 - 6)^2$

(e) $\dfrac{1-7}{3}$ (f) $\dfrac{{}^-6 \times 4}{8}$ (g) $\dfrac{{}^-9+5}{{}^-2}$ (h) $\dfrac{({}^-10)^2}{4}$

4 Find the missing number in each calculation.

(a) $9 + \blacksquare = 2$ (b) $4 \times \blacksquare = {}^-36$ (c) $\blacksquare \div 7 = {}^-3$ (d) $8 + {}^-3 - \blacksquare = {}^-1$

5 For each of these sequences, the first three terms and the rule are given.
Write down the next three terms of each sequence.

(a) 8 3 ${}^-2$ ...   Subtract 5 from the previous term.

(b) ${}^-27$ ${}^-20$ ${}^-13$ ...   Add 7 to the previous term.

(c) 5 ${}^-10$ 20 ...   Multiply the previous term by ${}^-2$.

6 Work out the value of each of these expressions when $n = {}^-5$.

(a) $2n + 3$ (b) $4 - n$ (c) $n^2 - 10$ (d) $3(n - 4)$

7 Here is a number machine chain.
Find the output for each of these inputs.

(a) 3 (b) ${}^-1$ (c) 5

8 Write these numbers in order of size, starting with the smallest.

3^2 2^3 $({}^-2)^3$ $({}^-4)^3$ $({}^-5)^2$ $({}^-1)^2$

9

A	N	R	I	E	S	K	T	G
${}^-4$	${}^-3$	${}^-2$	${}^-1$	0	1	2	3	4

Work out each calculation, use the code above and rearrange the letters
to find four sports.

(a) ${}^-3 + 2$ $1 \times {}^-3$ ${}^-1 \times {}^-2$ $3 - 4$ $7 - 3$ ${}^-1 + 2$

(b) ${}^-9 \div {}^-3$ ${}^-2 - {}^-2$ $1 - 5$ ${}^-6 \div 3$ ${}^-2 - 2$ ${}^-8 - {}^-10$

(c) ${}^-1 \times {}^-4$ $2 - 5$ ${}^-2 - {}^-1$ ${}^-1 + 4$ ${}^-2 \times 2$ ${}^-4 \div 2$ $5 - 3$

(d) ${}^-3 \times {}^-1$ ${}^-2 \div {}^-2$ ${}^-5 - {}^-1$ $3 \div {}^-3$ ${}^-6 + 3$ ${}^-6 \div {}^-3$ $({}^-2)^2$

37 Brackets

A Dividing an expression by a number

1 Find the missing number or expression in each statement.

(a) $\blacksquare \times 4n = 12n$ (b) $6y \times \blacksquare = 12y$ (c) $\blacksquare \times 2 = 10a$ (d) $3 \times \blacksquare = 21b$

2 Simplify each division.

(a) $\dfrac{8n}{2}$ (b) $\dfrac{9a}{3}$ (c) $\dfrac{25y}{5}$ (d) $\dfrac{16x}{4}$ (e) $\dfrac{28b}{7}$

3 Simplify each division.

(a) $\dfrac{6n + 14}{2}$ (b) $\dfrac{12k + 15}{3}$ (c) $\dfrac{4p + 8}{4}$ (d) $\dfrac{36 + 30w}{6}$

B Expressions with brackets
C Factorising an expression

1 There are three pairs of equivalent expressions here.
Pair them up and find the odd one left over.

| $5(c + 1)$ | $5(c + 2)$ | $5c + 50$ | $5c + 10$ | $5(c + 10)$ | $5c + 2$ | $5c + 5$ |

2 Multiply out the brackets in each of these expressions.

(a) $2(a + 3)$ (b) $4(b - 5)$ (c) $8(c - 2)$ (d) $5(4 + d)$ (e) $7(e - 3)$

3 Multiply out the brackets in each of these expressions.

(a) $5(2a + 3)$ (b) $2(3b - 4)$ (c) $7(2 + 3c)$ (d) $3(4d - 1)$ (e) $9(5e + 7)$

4 Find what is missing in each of these.

(a) $5(x - \blacksquare) = 5x - 20$ (b) $\blacksquare(3w + 5) = 6w + 10$

(c) $4(3v - \blacksquare) = 12v - 32$ (d) $4a + 6 = \blacksquare(2a + 3)$

(e) $15b - 12 = \blacksquare(5b - 4)$ (f) $40 + 70c = \blacksquare(4 + 7c)$

5 Factorise each of these expressions.

(a) $2p + 12$ (b) $3q + 6$ (c) $7r + 7$ (d) $7s - 14$ (e) $5t + 20$

(f) $4u + 10$ (g) $6v - 9$ (h) $10w + 5$ (i) $15x - 10$ (j) $12y + 2$

6 Factorise each of these completely.

(a) $8a + 4$ (b) $10b - 50$ (c) $16c - 12$ (d) $18d + 30$ (e) $24e - 32$

7

E	A	C	N	H	R	M	L	I	S
2	3	4	5	6	$x + 1$	$x + 2$	$2x + 1$	$2x + 3$	$3x + 2$

(a) Factorise the expressions below as far as you can.
Use the letters above to find three objects from a tool box.

(i) $10x + 15$ $\qquad$ $6x + 3$

(ii) $2x + 2$ $\qquad$ $3x + 6$ $\qquad$ $6x + 12$

(iii) $12x + 6$ $\qquad$ $6x + 4$ $\qquad$ $8x + 12$

(b) Make up a set of expressions to give the word CLEARS.

D Factorising more complex expressions

1 Copy each of these, filling in what is missing.

(a) $x(x + 5) = x^2 + \blacksquare$ $\qquad$ (b) $y(y - 7) = \blacksquare - 7y$ $\qquad$ (c) $z(3z - 2) = 3z^2 - \blacksquare$

2 Multiply out each of these expressions.

(a) $a(a + 9)$ $\qquad$ (b) $b(b - 6)$ $\qquad$ (c) $c(4 + c)$ $\qquad$ (d) $d(3 - d)$

(e) $e(3e + 5)$ $\qquad$ (f) $f(1 - 2f)$ $\qquad$ (g) $g(10g - 9)$ $\qquad$ (h) $h(7 + 5h)$

3 Multiply out each of these expressions.

(a) $2a(a + 3)$ $\qquad$ (b) $3b(b - 2)$ $\qquad$ (c) $5c(1 + c)$ $\qquad$ (d) $4d(5 - d)$

4 There are three pairs of equivalent expressions here, and one left over.
Find the three pairs and multiply out the one left over.

$c(2c + 1)$	$2c^2 + 5c$	$c(3c + 5)$	$2c^2 + c$	$3c^2 + 5c$	$c(c + 1)$	$c(2c + 5)$

5 Factorise each of these expressions.

(a) $s^2 + 4s$ $\qquad$ (b) $t^2 - 9t$ $\qquad$ (c) $7v + v^2$ $\qquad$ (d) $x^2 + 8x$

(e) $y^2 + 5y$ $\qquad$ (f) $12z + z^2$ $\qquad$ (g) $2u^2 + 3u$ $\qquad$ (h) $3w - 5w^2$

6 Expand these expressions.

(a) $3(c + d)$ $\qquad$ (b) $2(x - y)$ $\qquad$ (c) $5(2r + t)$ $\qquad$ (d) $3(x + 6y)$

(e) $4(3g - 2h)$ $\qquad$ (f) $2(4p - 7q)$ $\qquad$ (g) $6(5m + 4n)$ $\qquad$ (h) $5(2h - 10g)$

7 Find three pairs of equivalent expressions here.

$2x + 2y$	$2x + 4y$	$8x + 4y$	$2(x + 2y)$	$2(x + y)$	$4(2x + y)$

8 Factorise these expressions.

(a) $4u + 4v$ $\qquad$ (b) $2a + 8b$ $\qquad$ (c) $5m - 20n$ $\qquad$ (d) $9c + 12d$

E Adding an expression containing brackets
F Subtracting an expression containing brackets

1 Simplify these expressions.
   (a) $2(a + 3) + 4$
   (b) $8 + 5(b - 1)$
   (c) $3(c + 4) + 2c$
   (d) $6(d - 2) - d$
   (e) $7e + 2(4 - e)$
   (f) $5(f - 3) - 2f$

2 Simplify these expressions.
   (a) $3(2u + 1) + 5u$
   (b) $4 + 5(1 + 3v)$
   (c) $8(2w + 3) - 6w$
   (d) $5(4x + 2) - 10$
   (e) $8y + 2(4 - 3y)$
   (f) $10(5z - 3) - 19z$

3 Simplify these.
   (a) $3(c + 4) + 5(c + 1)$
   (b) $6(2 + 3d) + 2(d - 4)$
   (c) $5(3e + 1) + 2(7e - 4)$

4 Find four pairs of equivalent expressions.

$10 - (x + 4)$ $5 - (x + 1)$ $8 - (x - 6)$ $1 - (x - 1)$

$14 - x$ $2 - x$ $4 - x$ $6 - x$

5 Simplify these expressions.
   (a) $12 - (a + 1)$
   (b) $9 - (b - 2)$
   (c) $5c - (2c - 3)$
   (d) $9d - (5d + 7)$
   (e) $15 - (10 - 4e)$
   (f) $8f - (3 - 5f)$

6 Simplify each of these.
   (a) $15 - 2(m + 3)$
   (b) $9n - 3(n - 2)$
   (c) $7p - 5(4 - p)$
   (d) $6 - 4(q + 1)$
   (e) $15r - 2(r - 5)$
   (f) $9 - 2(4 - s)$

7 Simplify these expressions.
   (a) $4g + 5 - 2(g + 1)$
   (b) $6(h + 4) - 2(h + 3)$
   (c) $4(3 + j) - 2(j - 5)$
   (d) $5(k + 7) - 2(k - 3)$
   (e) $4(l + 2) - 2(l + 5)$
   (f) $3(5 - m) - 5(2 - m)$

8 There are three pairs of equivalent expressions here, and an odd one out.
   Which is the odd one out?

$(5x + 4) - (3x + 1)$ $3(2x + 1) - 2(2x - 1)$

$(5x + 1) - 2(x + 1)$ $(4x - 3) - (x - 2)$ $(4x - 3) - 2(x - 1)$

$3(3x + 2) - (7x + 1)$ $(6x + 1) - 2(2x - 1)$

9 Simplify these expressions.
   (a) $2(3n - 1) + 3(4n - 3)$ (b) $5(2x + 5) - 3(3x + 8)$ (c) $4(7k - 1) - 2(10k - 3)$

38 Pie charts

You need a pie chart scale or an angle measurer.

B Reading a pie chart: simple fractions and percentages

1 Some students were asked which type of house they lived in.
The pie chart shows the information.

(a) Which type of house was most common?

(b) Which type of house was least common?

(c) What percentage of the students lived in a terraced house?

(d) 120 students lived in a terraced house. How many students were asked altogether?

(e) (i) Measure the angle for semi-detached house.

(ii) What fraction of the students lived in a semi-detached house?

(iii) How many students lived in a semi-detached house?

(f) How many students lived in a flat?

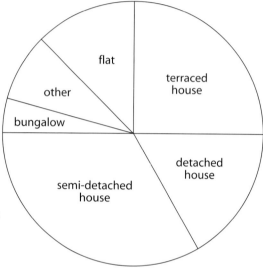

C Reading a pie chart: the unitary method

1 In a survey, 1800 people were asked which of four types of TV programme they liked best. Their replies are shown in the pie chart.

(a) How many people does 1° represent?

(b) (i) Measure the angle for quiz shows.

(ii) How many people liked quiz shows best?

(c) How many people liked soaps best?

(d) How many people liked films best?

2 Some senior citizens were asked about their favourite pets.

The results are shown in the pie chart.

(a) What fraction liked a dog best?

(b) 30 people chose dog.
How many people were asked altogether?

(c) How many people chose a cat as
their favourite pet?

(d) How many chose a budgie as
their favourite pet?

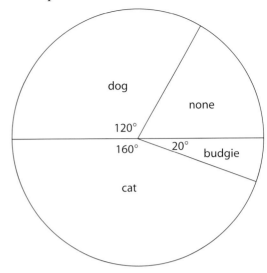

D Drawing a pie chart: angles

1 Joe recorded the hair colour of people in his class.

(a) How many people are there in his class?

(b) Work out what angle would represent one person
in a pie chart.

(c) What will be the angle for people with blonde hair?

(d) Work out the angles and draw the pie chart.
Label each sector.

Hair colour	Frequency
Blonde	5
Black	7
Brown	12
Red	2
Other	4

2 The table shows a summary of an investigation into where in the home
900 accidents occurred.

Where accident occurred	Kitchen	Stairs	Bathroom	Living room	Other
Frequency	400	225	150	90	35

Draw a clearly labelled pie chart to show this information.

3 In an investigation into accidents in the garden, 400 accidents were investigated.

(a) 80 accidents involved a spade.
In a pie chart showing the information, what is the angle
for accidents involving a spade?

(b) The angle for accidents involving lawnmowers was 135°.
How many of the accidents involved lawnmowers?

E Drawing a pie chart: percentages

1 In a survey 200 young people were asked about which sport they liked to watch on television.

The information is shown in the table.

Football	Motor racing	Snooker	Tennis	Cricket
90	64	12	24	10

(a) Draw a pie chart to illustrate this information. Label each sector clearly.

Some senior citizens were also asked the same question. This pie chart shows the results.

(b) State one way in which the results for young people and for senior citizens are similar.

(c) State one way in which the results for young people and for senior citizens are different.

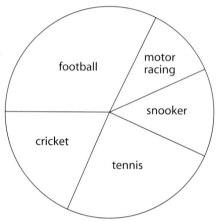

2 A company runs four types of family activity holiday.

The table shows the number of each type of holiday taken in one month.

Draw and label a pie chart to show this information. Show your working.

Type of holiday	Frequency
Skiing	115
Cycling	50
Walking	40
Boating	45

F Handling real data

1 The table shows how 600 people left the United Kingdom to travel abroad.

Draw and label a pie chart to illustrate this data.

Means of transport	Frequency
Channel Tunnel	84
Sea	151
Air	365

2 This table shows the total attendances at matches in the four English football leagues in the 2005/06 season.

Draw a pie chart to illustrate this data.

League	Total attendance (millions)
Premier League	12.9
Championship	9.7
League One	4.1
League Two	2.3
Total	29.0

39 Working with expressions 3

A Substituting into linear expressions

1 Copy this crossnumber grid.
Complete it using the clues below.
For the clues, $x = 7$, $y = 9$ and $z = 5$.

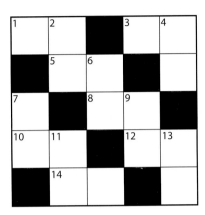

CLUES ACROSS	CLUES DOWN
1 $4z + 1$	**2** $x + 5$
3 $y + 2$	**4** $2y - 1$
5 $3y$	**6** $8(x + 2)$
8 $3(y - 1)$	**7** $8z - 9$
10 $10 + \dfrac{y}{3}$	**9** $11(z - 1)$
12 $8(y - 3)$	**11** $7z$
14 $4(9 + z)$	**13** $12z + 20$

2 Work out each of these when $x = 10$.

(a) $\dfrac{x + 4}{2}$ (b) $\dfrac{x}{2} + 4$ (c) $\dfrac{x - 4}{2}$ (d) $\dfrac{x}{5} - 2$ (e) $\dfrac{x - 16}{3}$

3 Evaluate each of these expressions when $x = {}^-1$.

(a) $3x$ (b) $x + 3$ (c) $2x + 7$ (d) $2(x + 7)$ (e) $3x + 1$

4 Evaluate each of these expressions when $x = {}^-6$.

(a) $\dfrac{x}{2}$ (b) $\dfrac{x}{3} - 1$ (c) $\dfrac{x}{2} + 8$ (d) $\dfrac{x + 16}{5}$ (e) $\dfrac{x + 2}{4}$

B Squares and cubes

1 Find the value of each expression when $n = 5$.

(a) n^2 (b) $n^2 - 4$ (c) n^3 (d) $3n^2$ (e) $2n^3$

2 Find the value of each expression when $y = 3$.

(a) $5y^2$ (b) $10 - y^2$ (c) $2y^3$ (d) $y^2 - 10$ (e) $40 - y^3$

3 Find the value of $k^2 + 1$ when $k = {}^-4$.

4 Use a calculator to find the value of each expression when $x = 24$.

(a) $2x^2$ (b) $\dfrac{x^2}{9}$ (c) $\dfrac{x^3}{72}$ (d) $3x^3$ (e) $500 - x^2$

C Using more than one letter

1 Given that $x = 4$ and $y = 3$, find the value of each of these expressions.

(a) $x + y$ (b) $x - y$ (c) $2(x + y)$ (d) $2x + 3y$ (e) $3x - 2y$

(f) xy (g) $xy - 5$ (h) $2xy$ (i) $3xy + 4$ (j) x^2

(k) y^2 (l) $x^2 + y^2$ (m) $x^2 - y^2$ (n) $x^2 + y$ (o) $x + y^2$

2 What is the value of each expression when $a = 2$, $b = 5$ and $c = 6$?

(a) $a + b + c$ (b) $a^2 + b^2$ (c) $ab + 3$ (d) $3ac$ (e) $3(a + b)$

(f) $4(c - a)$ (g) $a + 4b$ (h) $2(b - a)$ (i) $c^2 - a^2$ (j) $2ab - 9$

3 When $p = 2$, $q = 4$ and $r = 12$, evaluate these.

(a) $\dfrac{r}{q}$ (b) $\dfrac{r}{p} - 5$ (c) $\dfrac{q}{p} + 1$ (d) $\dfrac{r + q}{8}$ (e) $\dfrac{r - p}{5}$

4 What is the value of each expression when $a = {}^-10$ and $b = 5$?

(a) $a + 2$ (b) ab (c) $a^2 + b$ (d) $3(a + b)$ (e) $a - b$

(f) $\dfrac{a^2}{4}$ (g) $\dfrac{a}{b}$ (h) $3ab$ (i) $2a + 5b$ (j) $a + 2b$

(k) $\dfrac{a + b}{5}$ (l) $\dfrac{ab}{2}$ (m) $a^2 + b^2$ (n) $b - a$ (o) $\dfrac{a}{5} + b$

D Area and simplifying

1 Simplify each of these expressions.

(a) $3 \times 2k$ (b) $4 \times 3h$ (c) $5 \times 2g$ (d) $3m \times 8$ (e) $6p \times 7$

2 Simplify each of these expressions.

(a) $m \times n$ (b) $2f \times g$ (c) $h \times 5j$ (d) $3k \times 7l$ (e) $7p \times 5q$

(f) $5p \times 2p$ (g) $3n \times 4n$ (h) $10w \times w$ (i) $3b \times 3b$ (j) $k \times 6k$

3 Write down and simplify expressions for the areas of these rectangles.

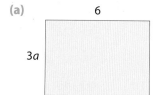

(a)   6,   3a

(b)   4m,   4n

(c)   6x,   5x

4 Write each of these in its simplest form.

(a) $pq + pq + 4pq$ (b) $8x^2 + 2x^2$ (c) $7ab - 3ab$

(d) $8k^2 - k^2$ (e) $8ab + ab - 6ab$ (f) $8x^2 + 2x^2 - 7x^2$

40 Multiplying and dividing fractions

A Finding a fraction of a quantity: fractional results 1

1 Five bars of chocolate are shared equally between four people.
How much chocolate does each person get?

2 Six pizzas are shared equally between four people.
How much pizza does each person get?

3 Work these out, writing your answers as mixed numbers.

   (a) $\frac{1}{3}$ of 10   (b) $\frac{1}{4}$ of 9   (c) $\frac{1}{5}$ of 11   (d) $\frac{1}{6}$ of 9

B Finding a fraction of a quantity: fractional results 2

1 Work these out. Give your answers as mixed numbers in their simplest form.

   (a) $\frac{1}{4}$ of 22   (b) $\frac{1}{8}$ of 20   (c) $\frac{1}{6}$ of 27   (d) $\frac{1}{3}$ of 11

2 Work out each answer and use the code to change it to a letter.

S	O	B	H	K	L	T	E	A	C	N	D
$\frac{2}{3}$	$\frac{3}{4}$	$1\frac{1}{2}$	$1\frac{2}{5}$	$1\frac{3}{5}$	$1\frac{4}{5}$	$2\frac{1}{3}$	$2\frac{1}{2}$	$2\frac{2}{3}$	$2\frac{3}{4}$	$3\frac{3}{4}$	$4\frac{3}{4}$

(You may need to simplify your answer.)

Then rearrange each set of letters to spell a piece of furniture.

   (a) $\frac{1}{4}$ of 10 $\frac{1}{8}$ of 12 $\frac{1}{4}$ of 19

   (b) $\frac{1}{10}$ of 18 $\frac{1}{3}$ of 8 $\frac{1}{2}$ of 5 $\frac{1}{3}$ of 7 $\frac{1}{2}$ of 3

   (c) $\frac{1}{6}$ of 14 $\frac{1}{6}$ of 15 $\frac{1}{8}$ of 22 $\frac{1}{5}$ of 7 $\frac{1}{3}$ of 2

3 Work these out. Give your answers as mixed numbers.

   (a) $\frac{3}{4}$ of 5   (b) $\frac{2}{5}$ of 3   (c) $\frac{2}{3}$ of 8   (d) $\frac{2}{7}$ of 5

4 Work out each answer and use the code to change it to a letter.

R	A	D	S	C	B	E	H	I	F	T	P
$\frac{6}{7}$	$1\frac{1}{5}$	$1\frac{1}{3}$	$1\frac{1}{2}$	$1\frac{2}{3}$	$2\frac{1}{4}$	$2\frac{2}{5}$	$2\frac{4}{5}$	$3\frac{1}{5}$	$3\frac{1}{3}$	$3\frac{3}{4}$	$6\frac{3}{4}$

Then rearrange each set of letters to spell an item of food.

   (a) $\frac{5}{6}$ of 2 $\frac{2}{7}$ of 3 $\frac{4}{5}$ of 4 $\frac{3}{5}$ of 4

   (b) $\frac{2}{5}$ of 6 $\frac{3}{8}$ of 6 $\frac{2}{3}$ of 5 $\frac{4}{5}$ of 3

   (c) $\frac{3}{10}$ of 5 $\frac{4}{5}$ of 4 $\frac{1}{4}$ of 27 $\frac{5}{9}$ of 3 $\frac{2}{5}$ of 7

C Dividing a unit fraction by a whole number

1 Work these out.

(a) $\frac{1}{4} \div 3$ (b) $\frac{1}{5} \div 2$ (c) $\frac{1}{2} \div 5$ (d) $\frac{1}{6} \div 3$

2 Matthew has $\frac{1}{3}$ of a cake.
He shares it equally with his brother and sister.
What fraction of the cake do they each get?

3 Work these out.

(a) $\frac{1}{3}$ of $\frac{1}{4}$ (b) $\frac{1}{4}$ of $\frac{1}{5}$ (c) $\frac{1}{5}$ of $\frac{1}{2}$ (d) $\frac{1}{2}$ of $\frac{1}{7}$

D Dividing a fraction by a whole number

1 Daniel has $\frac{3}{4}$ of a cake. He shares it equally with his friend Heather.
What fraction of the cake do they each get?

2 Work these out.

(a) $\frac{2}{5} \div 3$ (b) $\frac{2}{3} \div 5$ (c) $\frac{3}{4} \div 5$ (d) $\frac{4}{5} \div 3$

3 Work these out.

(a) $\frac{1}{2}$ of $\frac{3}{5}$ (b) $\frac{1}{4}$ of $\frac{3}{8}$ (c) $\frac{1}{5}$ of $\frac{2}{3}$ (d) $\frac{1}{3}$ of $\frac{2}{9}$

E Multiplying fractions

1 Work these out.

(a) $\frac{1}{2} \times \frac{1}{4}$ (b) $\frac{1}{3} \times \frac{1}{8}$ (c) $\frac{1}{4} \times \frac{3}{5}$ (d) $\frac{1}{2} \times \frac{3}{4}$

2 Work these out. Give each answer in its simplest form.

(a) $\frac{3}{5} \div 2$ (b) $\frac{1}{3}$ of $\frac{3}{5}$ (c) $\frac{1}{2}$ of $\frac{3}{8}$ (d) $\frac{1}{4} \times \frac{2}{7}$

(e) $\frac{1}{8}$ of $\frac{2}{5}$ (f) $\frac{5}{8} \div 3$ (g) $\frac{1}{10} \times \frac{5}{8}$ (h) $\frac{1}{6}$ of $\frac{3}{8}$

3 Put these calculations into pairs that give the same answer.
Write down the answer to each pair.

A $\frac{1}{10}$ of $\frac{5}{6}$ **B** $\frac{1}{3} \times \frac{5}{6}$ **C** $\frac{1}{2} \times \frac{5}{6}$ **D** $\frac{5}{6} \div 2$

E $\frac{5}{6} \div 3$ **F** $\frac{1}{4}$ of $\frac{5}{6}$ **G** $\frac{5}{6} \div 4$ **H** $\frac{1}{10} \times \frac{5}{6}$

41 Working with formulas 2

You need graph paper for section A.

A Formulas and graphs

1 Lend-a-Hand is a company offering to help with any job.

The formula they use to work out the charge for a job is $c = 6t + 5$.
c is the charge in £ and t is the time in hours.

(a) What is the charge for 2 hours of help?

(b) Copy and complete this table for Lend-a-Hand.

Time in hours (t)	1	2	3	4	5	6	7	8
Charge in £ (c)	11							

(c) Draw and label axes like those on the right.

Plot the points from your table.
Join them with a line.
Label the graph 'Lend-a-Hand'.

(d) Use your graph to estimate the charge for a time of $3\frac{1}{2}$ hours.

(e) Use your graph to estimate how much time you could buy for £50.

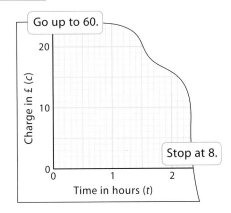

2 We're Cheaper is a rival company.

The formula they use to work out the charge for a job is $c = 7t$.
c is the charge in £ and t is the time in hours.

(a) What is the charge for 2 hours of help with We're Cheaper?

(b) Copy and complete this table for We're Cheaper.

Time in hours (t)	1	2	3	4	5	6	7	8
Charge in £ (c)			21					

(c) On the same axes that you used for question 1, plot the points from your table.
Join them with a straight line.
Label the graph 'We're Cheaper'.

(d) Estimate how much time you could buy for £50 with We're Cheaper.

(e) Use the graphs to say which company would be cheaper for $2\frac{1}{2}$ hours.
Explain your answer.

(f) How do the graphs show that both companies will charge the same for 5 hours?

B Forming and using formulas

1 A formula to work out the perimeter of a regular hexagon is

$$P = 6s$$

P is the perimeter of the regular hexagon and s is the length of one side.

(a) Calculate the perimeter of a regular hexagon where one side measures 12 cm.

(b) A regular hexagon has a perimeter of 120 cm.
What is the length of one side?

2 A clothes shop uses this arrow diagram to change UK shirt sizes to Continental ones.

UK shirt size → ×2 → +8 → Continental shirt size

(a) Change a UK shirt size of 14 to a Continental shirt size.

(b) Asif takes a UK shirt size of $16\frac{1}{2}$.
Find his Continental shirt size.

(c) Write down a formula that links UK shirt size (U) to Continental shirt size (C).

(d) What is the value of C when $U = 17$?

(e) Jean-Pierre takes a Continental shirt size of 40.
Form and solve an equation to find his UK shirt size.

3 To find the charge for mending burst pipes, a plumber uses the rule

Charge in £ = 20 × time taken in hours + 50

(a) How much will he charge for taking 3 hours to mend burst pipes?

(b) Write this as a formula connecting C and t.
C is the cost in pounds and t is the time taken in hours.

(c) Find the value of C when $t = 4$.

(d) The plumber charges £100 to mend some burst pipes.
Form and solve an equation to find how long he took.

4 A spa offers treatments such as massages and facials.
It works out the total cost of a day spent there using this rule.

£15 for each treatment + an entrance fee of £80

(a) Write this as a formula connecting C and n.
C is the cost in pounds and n is the number of treatments.

(b) Find the value of C when $n = 3$.

(c) Andrea spent a day at the spa and the total cost was £155.
How many treatments did she have?

C Forming and using expressions and formulas

1 Anthea has x ping-pong balls in a box.
Her mum buys her four more balls.
Write an expression for the number of ping-pong balls she has now.

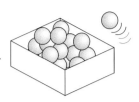

2 I have a roll of material m metres long.
I cut off n metres for a costume.
How much material is left?

3 A pencil costs n pence.

(a) Write down an expression for the cost of 10 pencils.

A biro costs 8 pence more than a pencil.

(b) Write an expression for the cost of 1 biro.

(c) Find and simplify an expression for the total cost of 1 biro and 10 pencils.

4 Paper cups cost c pence each.
Paper plates cost p pence each.

(a) Write an expression for the total cost of 1 cup and 1 plate.

(b) Write an expression for the total cost of 3 cups and 5 plates.

5 Yvonne buys x mugs at £3 each.
She pays for them with a £20 note.
She receives c pounds in change.
Write down a formula connecting c and x.

6 There are three piles of stones.

Pile A has x stones.
Pile B has twice as many stones as pile A.

(a) Write an expression for the number of stones in pile B.

Pile C has 6 stones fewer than pile A.

(b) Write an expression for the number of stones in pile C.

(c) Write and simplify an expression for the **total** number of stones in the three piles.

(d) The total number of stones in the three piles is 94.
Form an equation and solve it to find the number of stones in pile A.

Mixed practice 5

1 A cycling club uses this rule to find out how long a cycling tour takes.

$$T = \frac{d}{20} + 2 \quad (T \text{ is the time in hours and } d \text{ is the distance in kilometres.})$$

Use this rule to find the time taken for tours of

   (a) 80 km   (b) 100 km   (c) 50 km

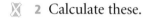 2 Calculate these.

   (a) $2 \times {}^-5$ (b) ${}^-3 \times {}^-4$ (c) ${}^-20 \div 4$ (d) $15 \div {}^-3$ (e) ${}^-14 \div {}^-2$

3 Multiply out the brackets in each of these expressions.

   (a) $2(x + 3)$ (b) $3(5n - 4)$ (c) $h(h + 3)$ (d) $3n(n - 5)$ (e) $5(a + 2b)$

4 This pie chart gives information about the audience for a science fiction film.

   (a) What percentage of the audience were men?

   (b) What fraction were women?

   (c) (i) Calculate the size of the angle for boys.

        (ii) What fraction of the audience were boys?

   (d) There were 300 people in the audience altogether. How many girls were in the audience?

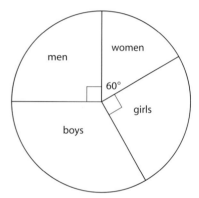

5 A sequence starts   2 8 14 20 ...

   (a) What is the rule for this sequence?

   (b) Write down the next two terms in this sequence.

6 Write down the negative square root of 25.

7 Simplify each of these expressions.

   (a) $2a + 4b + 3a + 7b$ (b) $6x + 2y - 4x + 3y$ (c) $4k + 2h + 3k - 6h$

8 (a) How many 44p stamps can you buy with £5?

   (b) James wants some 44p stamps.
       He buys 14 stamps and pays with a £10 note.
       How much change does he get?

   (c) Rachel buys some 44p stamps and pays with a £20 note.
       She gets £14.72 change.
       How many stamps does she buy?

9 What is the value of $\dfrac{n + 3}{2}$ when $n = 5$?

10 What does each person get when four buns are shared equally between three people?

11 Look at these patterns.

(a) How many dots will there be in pattern 4?

Pattern 1   Pattern 2   Pattern 3

(b) Copy and complete this table.

Pattern number	1	2	3	4	5
Number of dots					

(c) (i) Work out how many dots there will be in pattern 10.

  (ii) Explain how you worked out your answer.

(d) Which pattern will use exactly 152 dots?

12 A car hire company charges £24.50 per day, plus 12p per mile.
Anita hires a car from this company for two days and drives 232 miles.
Work out the total hire charge that Anita has to pay.

13 Find the value of each expression when $x = {}^{-}6$.

(a) $\dfrac{x}{2}$ (b) $x + 4$ (c) $2x + 15$ (d) $2x^2$ (e) $\dfrac{x^2}{9}$

14 A sequence starts   2   3   5   9   ...

The rule for the sequence is   Double previous number and subtract 1.

What is the next term in the sequence?

15 In June 2007, £1 was worth 2.05 US dollars.
How much (to 2 d.p.) was

(a) £125.75 worth in US dollars   (b) 350 US dollars worth in £

16 What is the value of each expression when $a = 5$, $b = 10$ and $c = {}^{-}2$?

(a) $a + b + c$ (b) $2a + 3c$ (c) $b^2 + c^2$ (d) $2bc$ (e) $\dfrac{b}{c} - 1$

17 Factorise each of these.

(a) $12n + 24$ (b) $4g - 14$ (c) $n^2 + 7n$ (d) $x^2 - 8x$ (e) $4a + 4b$

18 Work these out, giving each answer in its simplest form.

(a) $\frac{1}{4}$ of 10   (b) $\frac{2}{3}$ of 5   (c) $\frac{1}{3} \div 2$ (d) $\frac{1}{4} \times \frac{1}{5}$ (e) $\frac{3}{4} \times \frac{1}{9}$

19 In the Corner Café, a coffee costs 90p and a cup of tea 65p.
Ditta buys x coffees and y teas.
Write an expression for the total cost, in pence, of these drinks.

20 Simplify each of these.

(a) $5 \times 2x$ (b) $2a \times 5b$ (c) $3n \times 4n$ (d) $4gh + gh$ (e) $5k^2 - 3k^2$

42 Travel

You need squared paper in section B.

A Calculating speed

1 Find the speed, in metres per second, of
   (a) a sailfish swimming 900 m in 30 seconds
   (b) a cheetah running 1450 m in 50 seconds

2 Work out the average speed of these in km/h.
   (a) A train that goes 240 km in 3 hours
   (b) A plane that flies 2120 km in 4 hours

3 Calculate the average speed of these. State the units clearly in your answer.
   (a) A motorbike that goes 300 miles in 5 hours
   (b) A lion running 264 metres in 12 seconds

4 Work out the speed of each of these in km/h.
   (a) A coach that travels 15 km in half an hour
   (b) A car that travels 24 km in 15 minutes
   (c) A boat that sails 6 km in 20 minutes

5 Kate noted the reading on her mileometer at the start and end of a journey.

   Start   15702   End   15846

   (a) How long was the journey in miles?
   (b) The journey took 3 hours.
       What was her average speed for the journey?

B Distance–time graphs

1 This graph represents a walk.
   Copy and complete these statements about the walk.
   We walked at ___ km/h for the first ___ hours.
   We stopped for a break for ___ hour.
   It took us ___ hours to get back home.
   We walked a total of ___ km.

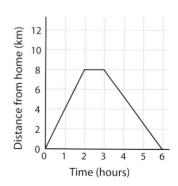

2 Azmat went for a cycle ride. This graph shows his journey.

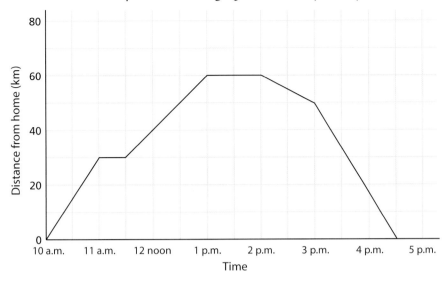

(a) What was Azmat's speed for the first hour?

(b) What happened at 11 a.m.?

(c) Between which two times was Azmat cycling slowest?

(d) Azmat stopped for lunch at 1 p.m.
     How far had he cycled before lunch?

(e) When did he start his journey home?

(f) What time did he arrive home?

3 Draw axes as in question 2, but with the time going to 6 p.m.

(a) Draw the graph to show this journey.

   • We left home at 10 a.m. and cycled at 25 km/h for two hours.

   • In the next hour we went faster and covered 30 km.

   • We then stopped for lunch for an hour.

   • After lunch we headed back and cycled steadily, arriving home at 6 p.m.

(b) What was the average speed on the return journey?

4 Maxine went for a walk.
   Her walk is represented by this graph.

   (a) On which section of the walk did she walk the slowest?

   (b) On which section of the walk did she walk the fastest?

   (c) What was her speed on section AB?

   (d) What was her speed on section CD?

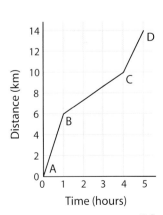

c Calculating distance and time

1 Connor walks at a steady speed of 5 km/h.
How long does he take to walk 20 km?

2 How far is each of these journeys?

  (a) A hawkmoth flies at 14 m/s for 30 seconds.

  (b) A greyhound runs at 17 m/s for 20 seconds.

  (c) A plane travels at 550 km/h for 3 hours.

  (d) A man runs at 8 km/h for 2 hours.

  (e) A train travels at 45 m.p.h. for 3 hours.

3 A car towing a caravan can drive at a maximum speed of 60 m.p.h. on a motorway.
At this speed, how far could it travel in

  (a) half an hour   (b) $2\frac{1}{2}$ hours   (c) $3\frac{1}{4}$ hours

4 How long would each of these journeys take?

  (a) A man walking at 5 km/h for 10 km

  (b) A woman cycling at 25 km/h for 100 km

  (c) A boat travelling at 6 km/h for 15 km

  (d) A motorbike travelling at 52 m.p.h. for 78 miles

5 A cyclist estimates that she can cycle at an average speed of 20 km/h.
How long should it take her to travel

  (a) 40 km   (b) 100 km   (c) 50 km   (d) 70 km

6 A coach travels at a steady speed of 50 m.p.h.
How far does it travel in $2\frac{1}{2}$ hours?

7 Scott leaves home at 8:45 a.m. and drives 125 miles to Leeds.
He drives at an average speed of 50 m.p.h.

  (a) How long does it take him to get to Leeds?

  (b) What time does he arrive in Leeds?

8 Work out the average speeds of these journeys.

  (a) Rita drives from Birmingham to Swindon in 2 hours 15 minutes.
       This is a journey of 90 miles.

  (b) Martin flies from Gatwick to Glasgow, a distance of 372 miles.
       The journey takes $1\frac{1}{2}$ hours.

  (c) Stacey gets a coach from Aberdeen to Hull, a distance of 360 miles.
       The journey takes 7 hours 30 minutes.

43 Graphs from rules

You need graph paper and squared paper.

A Patterns in coordinates

1 Look at the numbers in this table.
Which of the rules below is true?

x	0	1	2	3	4	5
y	0	4	8	12	16	20

$y = x + 4$ $x = 4$ $y = 4x$ $x + y = 4$

2 Here are four rules and four tables.
Which rule goes with which table?

$y = 3x$ $y = 5x + 2$ $y = 3x + 1$ $y = 5x + 3$

A

x	‑1	0	1	2	3	4
y	‑2	3	8	13	18	23

B

x	‑1	0	1	2	3	4
y	‑3	2	7	12	17	22

C

x	‑1	0	1	2	3	4
y	‑3	0	3	6	9	12

D

x	‑1	0	1	2	3	4
y	‑2	1	4	7	10	13

B Drawing a straight-line graph
C Including negative coordinates

1 (a) Copy and complete this table for the rule $y = x + 6$.

x	0	1	2	3	4	5
y						

(b) On axes like these, plot the points from the table.
Join the points with a line.

(c) What is the value of y when $x = 6$?

(d) Find y when $x = 3.5$.

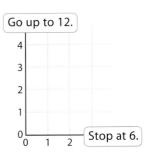

2 (a) Copy and complete this table for the equation $y = 2x + 2$.

x	0	1	2	3	4	5
y				8		

(b) On axes like these, plot the points from your table.
Join the points with a line.

(c) What is the value of y when $x = 2.5$?

(d) Copy and complete these coordinates for points on the line.

(i) $(1.3, \ldots\ldots)$ (ii) $(\ldots\ldots, 11)$

(iii) $(\ldots\ldots, 9.2)$ (iv) $(\ldots\ldots, 3.2)$

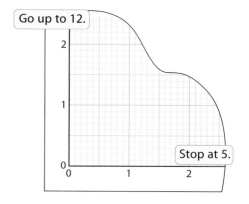

3 (a) Copy and complete this table for $y = 3x - 2$.

x	-2	-1	0	1	2	3
y	-8					

(b) On axes like these, plot the points from the table.
Join the points with a line.

(c) Copy and complete these coordinates for points on the line.

(i) $(0.5, \ldots\ldots)$ (ii) $(\ldots\ldots, 5.5)$

(iii) $(\ldots\ldots, 6.4)$ (iv) $(\ldots\ldots, {}^{-}6.2)$

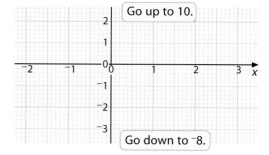

(d) (i) Copy and complete this table for $y = 2x - 3$.

x	-2	-1	0	1	2	3
y	-7					

(ii) On the same axes as you used in (b), plot the points from the table.
Join them with a line.

(e) What are the coordinates of the point where the lines cross?

4 (a) Copy and complete this table for $y = 3x + 1$.

x	-2	-1	0	1	2	3
y	-5					

(b) On axes like those in question 3, draw the graph of $y = 3x + 1$.

(c) What is the value of y when $x = 1.5$?

(d) Find the value of x when $y = 8.2$.

D Equations of horizontal and vertical lines

1 Copy this diagram on squared paper.

(a) Label each line with its equation.

(b) On the same diagram draw and label the line $y = x$.

(c) Write down the coordinates of the points where $y = x$ crosses each of the lines drawn.

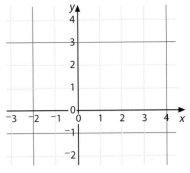

2 On squared paper, draw x- and y-axes both going from $^-5$ to 5.

(a) On your axes draw and label lines with these equations.

| $x = {}^-4$ | | $y = 2$ | | $x = 3$ | | $y = {}^-5$ |

(b) The four lines form a shape.
What is the name of the shape?

(c) Write down the coordinates of the corners of the shape.

E Implicit equations

1 (a) Copy and complete the table for $x + y = 12$.

x	0	2	4	6	8	10	12
y							

(b) On graph paper, draw axes with both x and y going from 0 to 14.
Plot the points from the table.
Draw and label the line $x + y = 12$.

(c) Copy and complete these coordinates for points on the line.

(i) $(4.5, \ldots\ldots)$ (ii) $(\ldots\ldots, 9.5)$

(d) Which of these points are on the line $x + y = 12$?

$(1.4, 10.6)$ $(1, 12)$ $(5.5, 6.5)$ $(3.9, 15.9)$

2 (a) Copy and complete this table for $4x + y = 20$.

x	0	1	2	3	4	5
y						

(b) On graph paper, draw axes with x from 0 to 5 and y from 0 to 20.
Draw and label the line $4x + y = 20$.

(c) From the graph, what is x when $y = 10$?

44 Working with coordinates

You need centimetre squared paper.

A Shapes on a grid
B Mid-points

1 The diagram shows two lines AB and BC and three points X, Y and Z.

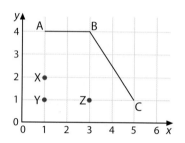

(a) What shape is made by joining up Z with A, B and C to make ABCZ?

(b) Write down the point that joins up with A, B and C to make a trapezium.

(c) What are the coordinates of the mid-point of BC?

2 The diagram shows three points, P, Q and R. Copy this diagram.

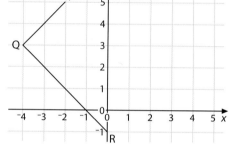

(a) What are the coordinates of P, Q and R?

(b) (i) Mark a new point S so that PQRS is a rectangle.

(ii) What are the coordinates of S?

(c) Draw in all the lines of symmetry of the rectangle.

(d) What is the order of rotation symmetry of the rectangle?

3 (a) Draw a grid on centimetre squared paper with x- and y-axes going from ⁻4 to 6. Mark the points A (6, 1), B (0, 5) and C (⁻2, 1).

(b) Mark the point D so that ABCD is a kite.

(c) What is the area of the kite?

(d) (i) Mark the mid-point of each side of the kite. Join the mid-points to make a new quadrilateral.

(ii) What type of quadrilateral is the new one?

4 (a) Draw a grid with x- and y-axes going from ⁻4 to 6. Mark the points P (⁻4, 0), Q (⁻4, 2) and R (4, 6).

(b) (i) Mark the point S so that PQRS is a trapezium with one line of symmetry.

(ii) What is the equation of the line of symmetry?

(c) (i) Mark the mid-point of each side of the trapezium. Join the mid-points to make a new quadrilateral.

(ii) What type of quadrilateral is the new one?

C Reflection
D Rotation

1 (a) Which shape is the image of A
after reflection in the line $y = 2$?

(b) Describe the reflections that take

   (i) shape A to shape B

   (ii) shape C to shape B

(c) What is the image of the point $(2, 3)$
after reflection in the line $x = 1$?

(d) What is the image of the point $(^-3, ^-2)$
after reflection in the line $y = 2$?

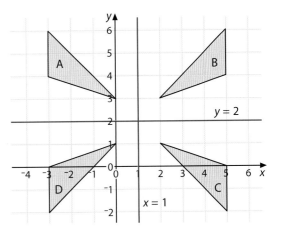

2 Copy the diagram below.

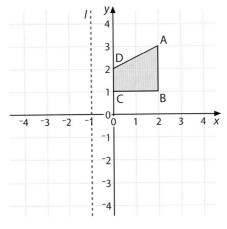

(a) (i) Draw the reflection of shape ABCD in
the mirror line l.

   (ii) What are the coordinates of the
image of point A?

(b) (i) Show the image of shape ABCD after
a rotation of 90° clockwise about $(0, 0)$.

   (ii) What are the coordinates of the image
of point B after this rotation?

(c) Show the image of shape ABCD after a
rotation of 180° about $(^-1, 0)$.

3 (a) Draw a grid with x- and y-axes going from $^-6$ to 6.
Mark and join the points $(2, 2)$, $(5, 2)$ and $(5, 4)$ to make a triangle.
Label the triangle W.

(b) Rotate shape W 90° anticlockwise about $(0, 0)$.
Label the image X.

(c) Rotate shape W 180° about $(0, 0)$.
Label the image Y.

(d) Reflect shape W in the x-axis.
Label the image Z.

(e) Describe the transformation that takes

   (i) shape Y to shape Z

   (ii) shape X to shape Y

45 Trial and improvement

A Searching for whole numbers

1 When two numbers are added together, the answer is 60.
When the same two numbers are multiplied together, the answer is 864.
What are the two numbers?

2 Find a cube number number between 300 and 400.

3 (a) Find a pair of consecutive numbers that multiply together to make 2070.

(b) Find two consecutive **odd** numbers that multiply together to make 5475.

B Searching for decimals

1 Two numbers differ by 0.5 and multiply to make 264.
Find the two numbers.

2 Two numbers add to make 17 and multiply to make 61.36.
Find the two numbers.

C Searching for approximate values

1 The area of a rectangle is 60 cm².
The length is 3 cm longer than the width.

width + 3

width

Copy and complete this table to find the width to one decimal place.

Width	Width + 3 (length)	Area (target 60 cm²)	Result too small	too big
4	7	28	✓	
5				

2 The volume of a cube is 100 cm³.

Copy and complete this table to find the length of an edge of the cube, correct to one decimal place.

Length of edge	Volume (target 100 cm³)	Result too small	too big
5	125		✓

46 Constructions

You need a pair of compasses and an angle measurer.

A **Drawing a triangle using lengths**
B **Drawing a triangle using angles**
C **Drawing a triangle using two sides and an angle**

1 For each of the triangles sketched here,

   • make an accurate drawing

   • measure the angle or length marked with a letter

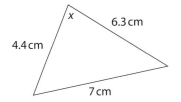   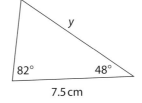   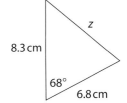

2 (a) Make an accurate drawing of a triangle ABC, in which
         AB = 10.9 cm, AC = 6.0 cm and BC = 9.1 cm.

   (b) What type of triangle is ABC?

   (c) Calculate the area of triangle ABC, giving your answer in cm² to 1 d.p.

3 The line XZ is 5 cm long.
   It is to be used as the base of a triangle XYZ.

   Say whether each of these pairs of angles
   could be used to complete the triangle.

   (a) YXZ = 55° and YZX = 125°

   (b) YXZ = 45° and YZX = 100°

   (c) YXZ = 75° and YZX = 110°

4 The line PR is 6 cm long.
   It is to be used as the base of a triangle PQR.

   Say whether each of the following pairs of sides
   could be used to complete the triangle.

   (a) PQ = 7 cm and RQ = 3 cm

   (b) PQ = 3 cm and RQ = 2 cm

   (c) PQ = 9 cm and RQ = 2 cm

5 This sketch shows some measurements for a triangle.
Make accurate drawings of **two different** triangles that
have these measurements.

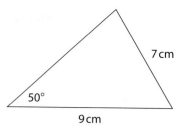

6 (a) Make an accurate drawing of
the quadrilateral sketched here.

(b) What special type of quadrilateral is it?

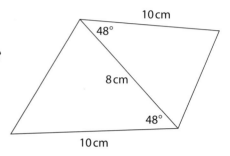

7 (a) Make an accurate drawing of
the quadrilateral sketched here.

(b) What special type of quadrilateral is it?

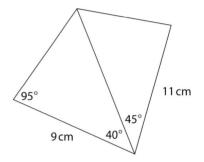

D Scale drawings

1 This is a designer's sketch for a side view of a flower bowl.

(a) Draw an accurate scale drawing of the side view
using a scale where 1 cm represents 2 cm.

(b) From your scale drawing find

   (i) d, the distance across the top of the actual bowl

   (ii) h, the height of the actual bowl

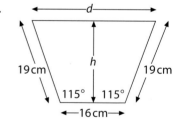

2 (a) Draw an accurate plan of this park,
using a scale of 1 cm to 10 m.

(b) There are two straight paths in the park,
one from Main Gate to Honeysuckle Gate
and the other from Archway to Dewdrop Gap.

What is the length, in metres, of the longer path?

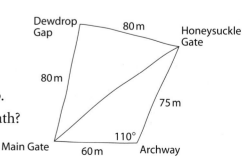

Mixed practice 6

You need a pair of compasses, an angle measurer, graph paper and centimetre squared paper.

1 This table shows the distances in miles between some places in Scotland.

 (a) How far is it between Aberdeen and Glasgow?

 (b) Madge drove from Inverness to Aberdeen.
 The journey took 2 hours.
 What was her average speed?

 (c) Gordon drove from Perth to Fort William.
 It took him $2\frac{1}{2}$ hours.
 What was his average speed?

	Aberdeen	Fort William	Glasgow	Inverness	Perth
157					
147	102				
106	65	173			
86	105	61	114		

2 (a) Draw a grid on centimetre squared paper with x- and y-axes going from ⁻4 to 4.
 Plot the points A (3, 1), B (2, 2) and C (3, 4).

 (b) Mark the point D so that ABCD is a kite.

 (c) What are the coordinates of the mid-point of BC?

 (d) Show the image of the shape ABCD after reflection in the line $x = 1$.

 (e) Show the image of the shape ABCD after a quarter turn clockwise about (0, 0).

3 Copy this diagram on to squared paper.

 (a) Label each line shown in red with its equation.

 (b) Add the graph of $x = 2$ to your diagram.

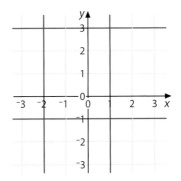

4 Cathy's paintings are all 4 cm taller than they are wide.
She wants to make a painting with an area of 1000 cm².

Width	Width + 4 (length)	Area (target 1000 cm²)	Result too small	too big
20	24	480	✓	

Copy and complete this table to find the width correct to one decimal place.

5 Jane walks for 4 hours at an average speed of 3 m.p.h.
How far does she walk?

6 Triangle ABC has sides AB = 6 cm, BC = 8 cm and AC = 4 cm.

    (a) Using a ruler and compasses only, make an accurate drawing of the triangle.

    (b) Measure and write down the size of the obtuse angle in the triangle.

7 How long, in hours and minutes, does it take to drive 195 miles at an average speed of 60 m.p.h?

8 (a) Copy and complete the table of values for $y = 4x - 1$.

x	⁻1	0	1	2
y		⁻1		

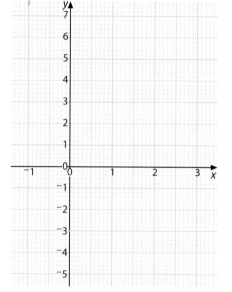

    (b) On a grid like this, draw the graph of $y = 4x - 1$.

    (c) Use your graph to find

        (i) the value of y when $x = {}^-0.5$

        (ii) the value of x when $y = 5$

    (d) Copy and complete the table of values for $x + y = 2$.

x	⁻1	0	1	2	3
y	3				

    (e) Add the graph of $x + y = 2$ to your diagram.

    (f) What are the coordinates of the point where the two lines cross?

9 Fraser went for a cycle ride.
His ride is represented by this graph.

    (a) How far was he from home after 1 hour?

    (b) What was his average speed on the part of his ride represented by section AB?

    (c) What happened on the part of his ride represented by section CD?

    (d) What was his average speed on the part of his ride represented by section DE?

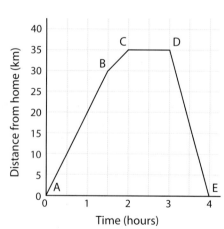

10 Find the cube root of 15 625.